The Ohio Free Will Baptist Pulpit

Compiled

By

Dr. Alton E. Loveless

The Ohio Free Will Baptist Pulpit

Copyright 2014

By

Dr. Alton E. Loveless

ISBN 13: 978-0692342824

All rights reserved

No part of this book may be reproduced or transmitted in any form or by any means, electronic or mechanical, including photocopying, recording, or by any information storage and retrieval system, without permission in writing from the copyright owner.

This book was printed in the United States of America.

To order additional copies of this book, contact:

FWB Publications
1006 Rayme Drive
Columbus, Ohio 43207
740--777-1944

Amazon.com

Published by
FWB Publications

FWB

Introduction

For many years I have listened to great preaching and have concluded that Ohio Free Will Baptist preachers are among some of the best I have heard during my 60 years of ministry.

I count it an honor to include a few messages from the men in this book, and their permission for me to publish their sermons.

It is my desire to publish other volumes of sermon books from additional ministers. I thank the Lord for the inspiration and knowledge He has given His messengers and the Holy Spirit filled preaching.

Alton E. Loveless

Cover Photo

Brush Creek Free Will Baptist Church

The Ohio Free Will Baptist Pulpit

Table of Contents

I Find No Fault In Him 7
    Edwin Hayes, State Executive-Secretary

America Needs Revival 15
    Bill Hayes, Pastor: Hill View FWB, Reynoldsburg

Love 27
    Calvin Evans, Founder Evangelism Outreach, Pedro

The Promise Of Eternal Life 37
    Mark Price, Pastor: Porter FWB, Slocum Station

Nevertheless The Enemy Is Strong 49
    Michael J. Gillen JD, Minister, Attorney, Assn. Clerk

Reviewing The Present 57
    Alton E. Loveless, Retired Pastor, Denominational Officer

The Discovery Of Authority 95
    Shawn Beauchamp, Pastor: Canaanland FWB, Grove City

The Letters To The Seven Churches 111
    Robert Prichard, Pastor: Cleveland FWB, Cleveland

Things That Hinder Our Prayers 129
    Tom Dooley, Pastor: First FWB, Austintown

When Is A Preacher A Failure? 135
    Tim Stout, Pastor: Heritage FWB, Columbus

Hold On! 149
    Louis Nettleton, Pastor: Williams Road FWB, Columbus

The Poor Wise Man And Other Forgotten Hero's 157
    Mike Mounts, Pastor: Harrison FWB, Minford

How To Spoil Everyone's Day And Ruin Your Life 167
    Aaron Reid, Pastor: Sciotodale FWB, Wheelersburg

THE UNSINKABLE SHIP **181**
　FREDDY DUTTON, FULL-TIME EVANGELIST, COLUMBUS
WHY I AM A FREE WILL BAPTISTS **189**
　EDWIN HAYES, STATE EXECUTIVE-SECRETARY

1

I Find No Fault in Him
John 18:38-19:6

Edwin Hayes
Executive-Secretary – Ohio Association of Free Will Baptists

Have you ever thought about what your relationships in life are based on? On what do they stand? It really has to be one of two things-love or perfection. Think about it, what are your friendships based on love or perfection? What about your marriage, love or perfection? Of course, since we are imperfect I have found that our relationships with others cannot be based on perfection but on love. We put up with each other's shortcomings because we love them. Love truly *"covers a multitude of sins."*

But when it comes to our relationship with God it is based on both perfection and love. God is perfect and everything and everyone who comes before Him must be perfect. At the end of the Sermon on the Mount Jesus said for us to be perfect, as His heavenly Father is perfect. This presents to us a problem. As we look at ourselves we do not see perfection, we only see imperfection, faults, failures and sin. How can we ever have a relationship with a Holy God? Many times we attempt to bring God down to our level and allow Him to become too "common" to us and we develop the wrong concept of God. We think He is like us! God is not like us!

When Jesus was brought before Pilate there were many charges against Him. Rebellion, sedition, making Himself a rival to the Roman Emperor were stated against Him. After Pilate spent some time with Christ, he presented Him before the crowd with this verdict, *"I find no fault in him:"* Three times in fact! I have inspected Him and have come to the conclusion that He has done nothing that would warrant His death. No fault in Him! There have been many that have investigated Jesus over the years. I don't know of a figure in human history that has had the scrutiny that Jesus has and yet when people do they can honestly say, *"I find no fault in Him."*

The only way to have a relationship with a Holy God is to stand with His Perfect Son, Jesus and take on His perfection before the Father. This is the only way we can live up to the perfection called for in the Sermon on the Mount.

I would like to examine the subject of perfection and how it relates to Christ and how it relates to us.

The Old Testament Demands Perfection
In the Old Testament God lays the groundwork for man's salvation. He shows us that only His plan that will save us--not good works, not religion, not man's best. Only His perfection will do.

Throughout these Scriptures, God shows us examples of His perfection.

The Old Testament <u>Priest</u> pictures perfection by his qualifications, his clothing and his behavior. This is why severe punishment was given to priests who rebelled against God. Strange fire was offered by Aaron's sons, Nadab and Abihu and they were consumed by God. Lev. 10:1-2) Eli's sons, Hophni and Phinehes were slain because of their lewd behavior. (I Samuel 4:11)

The Old Testament <u>Sacrifices</u> picture perfection. The sacrifices were to be without spot or blemish. They were to be the first and the best. The priests would inspect them to make sure they were. Only then could the sacrifices be accepted. The Lord would then have a sweet smelling savor rising up to Him. The Lord noticed when they were not the best! (Malachi 1)

The sacrifice's blood was to be shed to show us the supreme cost of sin and the holiness of God. On the day the temple was dedicated, 22,000 oxen and 120,000 sheep were sacrificed! (I Kings 8:63) Imagine all that blood flowing? It would surely draw man's attention to his imperfection. Sin must be paid for and God's standard is perfection.

The Old Testament <u>Law</u> pictures perfection. This is God's perfect moral compass. The Ten Commandments given in Exodus 20:1-11 cannot be improved on, even in the modern day in which we live!

The Old Testament <u>Tabernacle</u> pictures perfection. The Ark of the Covenant which resided in the tabernacle signified the very presence of God. That is why the special care in moving it. It was only carried by Levites by poles. (Numbers. 3:31) Uzzah was judged severely when Israel neglected this command. (II Samuel 6:6-7)

The Holy of Holies of the Tabernacle was so perfect that men were not welcome there!
The Old Testament leaves no question-God's standard is not man's best, it is perfection!

The New Testament Describes Perfection
If you want to see perfection, we must look at Christ! His whole life exhibits perfection.

He was perfect in His <u>Birth</u>. According to the Scriptures, He, unlike any other man was born of a virgin in the little village of Bethlehem.

He was perfect In His <u>Baptism</u>. When John baptized Jesus the heavens opened and the voice of God proclaimed *"This is my beloved Son in whom I am well pleased."* (Matthew 3:14-17)

He was perfect in His <u>Introduction.</u> John the Baptist introduced Jesus in this way, *"Behold the Lamb of God which taketh away the sin of the world."* (John 1:29)

He was perfect in His <u>Temptation</u> (Matthew 4) Satan threw every temptation possible at Jesus, yet Jesus resisted every attempt. In John 8:46 He asks the question, *"Which of you convinceth me of sin?"* The answer of course was no one!

He was perfect in His <u>Teaching</u>. The Sermon on the Mount is God's perfect plan for His Kingdom. Men exclaimed that Jesus taught like no other man!

He was perfect in His <u>Confrontations</u>. The Pharisees, Sadducees, and Herodian's all tried to find fault with Jesus but to no avail. Every time they confronted Him they walked away completely confounded.

He was perfect in His <u>Garden</u>. It was there He perfectly submitted to the will of His Father (Luke 22:42)

He was perfect in His <u>Trials</u>. No fault was found in Him in any of the trials He faced. Honestly, all the officials really didn't know what to do with Him!

He was perfect on His <u>Cross</u>. So much so that a thief recognized His perfection and asked Him for salvation! (Luke 23: 42)

He was perfect in His <u>Death</u>. Only when His mission was accomplished, He cried, *"It is finished"* (John 19:30) and the veil of the temple which guarded the Holy of Holies rent in two. (Matthew 27:51) signifying that Jesus' death had paid for man's entrance into the presence of God. When a Roman soldier saw this, he exclaimed, *"Truly this was the Son of God."* (Matthew 27:54)

He was perfect in His <u>Resurrection</u>. On the third day, He conquered death, hell and the grave as He triumphantly arose. Death could not hold Him!

He was perfect in His <u>Commission</u>. He told the disciples to take His marvelous message of salvation to all nations. (Matthew 28:19-20)

He was perfect in His <u>Ascension.</u> The heavens received the perfect Savior and He took His place at the Father's right hand. (Acts 1:8-9) (I Timothy 3:16)

He is perfect in His <u>Mediation</u>. Romans 8 asks these questions for those found for whom Christ mediates: *"Who is he that can condemneth?"* (vs. 34) *"Who can lay anything to the charge of God's elect?"* (vs.33.) The answer, of course is no one! *"There is one mediator between God and man, the man Christ Jesus."* (I Timothy 2:5)

Remember the old Perry Mason or Matlock TV shows. You just knew that whoever they would represent, that in the end they would prevail. Jesus is greater than Perry Mason or Matlock in that He never loses as case! We can have perfect confidence in Him

He is perfect in His <u>Return</u>. All issues will be settled when Jesus comes again. We can confidently await the day when all wrongs will be made right!

Truly we echo the words of Pilate, *"I find no fault in him!"* Even today the most severe skeptics still respect Him.

The Church Displays His Perfection

Think of where you were when you met Christ. Remember when Jesus first met Simon Peter He expressed His plans for him. He said to him, *" Thou art Simon the son of Jona: thou shalt be called Cephas"*(John 1:42) As Simon the rough fisherman stood before Jesus that day, he was told that He was going to make him much more than he was. He was going to be greatly used of the Lord for His purposes.

We know that Simon Peter had many ups and downs in his life, but walking with Christ, and going through the process the Lord did for him what He said He would. Peter became a leader in the church, a mature apostle with a rock like faith who would give his life for Jesus. What a change in Simon Peter!

You see, when Jesus sees us today, He just doesn't see what we are, and He sees what we can be. Here is how the process works.

When we come to Him, in His grace He saves us from an awful fate! We are accepted in the beloved. (Ephesians 1:6) We then stand in His righteousness alone. Just as Jesus accepted Peter even after he failed Him, (John 21) He accepts us into His family.

But He is not through with us there! He not only saves us but He sanctifies us as well! As Philippians 1:6 says *"Being confident of this very thing, that he which hath begun a good work in you will perform it until the day of Jesus Christ."* He is working in our lives right now to make us like Him!

One day the job will be complete This is expressed in I John 3:2 *"Beloved now we are the sons of God, and it doth not yet appear what we shall be, but we know when he shall appear we shall be like him; for we shall see him as he is"*

That day Jesus will bring us before the Father to be inspected. He will be able to say "I find no fault in you." He will not see my faults that day! He will not see my failures that day! He will not see my shortcomings that day! He will not see my sin that day! This world doesn't think much of the Church. In their eyes, we may be small, but not the Lord! In His eyes, we are priceless!

I like the last verse of this great old song *"When He shall come with trumpet sound, O may I then in Him be found; Dressed in His righteousness alone, Faultless to stand before the throne. On Christ the solid Rock I stand; All other ground is sinking sand, All other ground is sinking sand."*

Christ has freed us from our imperfect state and allowed us to live. Let's take this great freedom and hope that we have in Him and live up to the standing He has given us. One day we will stand with Jesus in perfection. Another songwriter put it this way *"And when before the throne I stand in Him complete, Jesus died my soul to save my lips will still repeat. Jesus paid it all, all to Him I owe; Sin had left a crimson stain, He washed it white as snow."*

2
America Needs Revival
2 Timothy 4

Bill Hayes
Pastor Hill View FWB church – President Impulse Missions

6 For I am now ready to be offered, and the time of my departure is at hand.

7 I have fought a good fight, I have finished my course, I have kept the faith:

8 Henceforth there is laid up for me a crown of righteousness, which the Lord, the righteous judge, shall give me at that day: and not to me only, but unto all them also that love his appearing.

We are living in perilous times. Every day, I am reminded of the words of scripture as I see them being fulfilled at break-neck speed. Hundreds of years of prophecy is being fulfilled before our very eyes and it doesn't look good for the church in America.

CHURCH IN AMERICA

- 85% of churches are stuck or in decline
- On average, 4,000 churches a year are closing.
- Church attendance is down 50% from the 1950's here in the US.
- Only around 20% of Americans regularly attend church

Kathy Chiero (Kiro), Christian talk radio host of The Sitting Room, stated this past Sunday that the number of people regularly attending church peeked in the mid-1950's at about 59%. Now, that number has declined to just over 20% - people who regularly attend church. Some polls report it's closer to 17%.

Well-known church researcher and author Thom Rainer notes that "the failure of churches to keep up with the population growth is one of the Church's greatest issues heading into the future." The increase in churches is only 1/4 of what's needed to keep up with population growth. It is statistically predicted that by 2050, regular church attendance in America will be around 11%.

Mid-sized churches (100-300 people) are shrinking; the smallest churches and largest churches are the ones growing.

The number of church members classified as inactive is estimated to be around 40-60%.

The church in America appears to be dying. Yet, world-wide, we see a different picture.

In China and Africa, the church is growing. Within 10-15 years, the number of people regularly attending church in Communist China will eclipse the number of people regularly attending church in the United States. Yet, in the places where the church is growing, it's hard to go to church, worship openly, and profess you are a Christian. And persecution is prevalent.

In America,

Poll Results Of The Top 4 Reasons People Say They Avoid Church

1. I feel judged (87%) (91% say we're anti-homosexual)
2. I don't want to be lectured
3. Church people are hypocrites
4. God is irrelevant

I don't know, but I would say if you took a poll in Rome during the time of Paul, or during the reformation, or in the 1960's in America, the results might prove to be similar.

Jesus wasn't popular. In fact, He was pretty much alone by the time He went to the cross.

It's always been that way. We've lived with those statistical disadvantages since the Garden of Eden.

In John 16, Jesus tells us that the role of the Holy Spirit after His ascension would be to convict the world of Sin, Righteousness, and _____ yes, Judgment.

Should we make it easier, more comfortable, and more inviting? Should we change our stand on morals or lighten the load of doctrine in our preaching and teaching so people would feel less-judged?

I understand how daunting and uncomfortable it is for a non-believer to attend a church service. We members and attenders should make guests feel welcome and loved, regardless of who they are, what they wear, or the sins they are involved in.

But, we can't change our message and, we won't. And, I say that unapologetically.

Yes, AMERICA NEEDS REVIVAL.

In our culture and "ME" generation, mankind is becoming more and more selfish. Paganism is rampant. Baal is being worshiped and her name is materialism. Convenience is another god we serve and she brings with her un-holiness and irreverence. We praise ourselves for what we have and deny the power and praise our Creator God deserves. Families are in disarray because its Biblical identity is being rebelled against.

Homosexuality, bisexuality, bestiality, transgender, transvestites, as well as numerous other inappropriate and unbiblical relationships are ripping a hole in the fuselage of America and bringing her down.

Righteousness exalts a nation but sin is a reproach to any people. –BUT- Blessed is the nation whose God is the Lord...

Yet, we decline. We decline to be thankful, hardworking, truthful and honest and we fight for entitlements by robbing others that are good. So we are in decline as a nation and the declining church is its byproduct.

Mankind is arrogant. We love ourselves. We love our pleasures, and we HATE GOD. We, who have been blessed by God, stand accused as traitors against the hand of blessing.

Oh, we say we're godly. We say we believe, but it's all just a form – a template to make us look good and cover our hypocrisy. There is no divine power in us and, therefore, there is no godliness in us as well. We wear the lipstick of our master the Devil to try and cover up who we really are. We want to retain the blessings of the almighty by trying to hide the diseased pork in our hearts.

John 8:44 says, "Ye are of your father the devil, and the lusts of your father ye will do. He was a murderer from the beginning, and abode not in the truth, because there is no truth in him."

Games and fancies are more important and have become our idols. Too many, everything we love comes before God and His church – the church Christ died for.

Some in the church have fed their lusts by presenting an easy gospel. The truth is being resisted by many in the Christian community for the sake of ease and the profit of those who preach.

The church is filled with people like Jannes and Jambres who want to adjust the truth to get their way. The theologians desire to know more of God has turned into knowing more than God – and that, my friends, is impossible. They wrestle with scripture and malign Holy words to fit into their ideology and philosophy where nothing is sin anymore and we are creating a heaven on earth.

We forget that all of those that will live godly in Christ shall suffer persecution.

And yet, it is creeping into many churches – this damnable new-age philosophy. Even we as pastors sometimes forget that it is doctrine, our manner of life, our purpose, faith, longsuffering, charity, and patience that should characterize our ministry as well as that of each believer. When we should continue in the teachings of scripture that many of us have been taught from our youth, we instill doubt in the heart of church-goers and cause them to believe a lie.

Do you not remember that scripture is immutable, unchangeable, inspired by God, and is not only our rule of faith and practice but an instrument, wielded by the man of God and actuated by the Holy Spirit of God?

Have we forgotten that it is the word of God that brings life? It is the word of God that takes those who are enslaved by the Devil and sets them free? It is Holy Spirit empowered Holy Scripture that releases the bonds of alcoholism and drug addiction and breaks the chains of sexual sins, abuse, and materialism. Not a lesson on love. Not a teaching that makes me feel good about myself.

Yet pulpiteers rub and smear the words of our Savior and make them impotent.

Yes, feeding the poor is good, and Godly, and assisting those in need of physical help commendable. But it is not the message of Christ. The message of Christ is the cross. The message of Christ is repentance. The message of Christ is forgiveness of sins. The message of Christ is salvation. The message of Christ is good deeds born out of salvation - not for salvation. Teaching a man to fish and giving him a fishing pole may keep him from hunger but it won't keep him from Hell.

God forbid that we should glory. None of us should glory in our sermons, our eloquence, our giving to the poor, our serving our community. But God forbid that any of us should glory, save in the cross of our Lord Jesus Christ...

AMERICA NEEDS REVIVAL!

We have been warned. We are in the time of unsound doctrine and itching ears. Lust fills many pulpits and pews and inept teaching has replaced truth.

We were told, were we not? Haven't you heard it before? Have you read chapter 3 of Paul's second letter to Timothy where all of these things were prophesied?

Big church – little church; music; church polity; missions; money; pastoral authority. We have hid behind plastic walls of diversion and doctrinal ease at the expense of burning souls in a real Hell and it's not a Hell on earth. There is no real Hell on earth.

This ship in America is sinking and we don't have time to rearrange the deck chairs or make our beds. We're sinking. Americans are dying spiritually.

I suggest to you that America needs prophets today like Elijah who will go against the establishment and say, "If the Lord be God, follow Him. But if Baal, then follow him."

We need pulpits with men who will "Preach the Word" all the time – in their sermons and in their lifestyles. We need pastors who will not be tempted by the masses. Men who will preach sound doctrine. Men not corrupted by a lust for financial prosperity. Men opposed to materialism. We need men who recognize the effect of sin on our Savior and the magnanimous cost to Heaven.

We need men and women crowned with righteousness and good deeds who will not be afraid to stand and share the message of the cross. Men and women who will stand for the truth whatever is costs; stand for the sinner as a watchman on the wall; stand for the declining Christian plucking them out of the fire.

AMERICA NEEDS REVIVAL!

American politics and politicians are tainted. Their desire has shifted from the good of the people to the lust of the flesh.

America is falling, sin is rampant, and those in government at all levels are using a one gallon bucket to get rid of the water of a titanic disaster. We need to pray for the men and women who govern our nation. Freedom weeps and it is because God is ignored. The lack of godliness in our government and the insatiable desire of many to erase God from our history, present, and future is destroying us.

William Penn said "If we will not be governed by God, we must be governed by tyrants."

Wrong rules the land. Justice and equality has been replaced by a lust for power and greed. People have been replaced with poles and policy. Life, liberty, and the pursuit of happiness is being crushed by materialism and debauchery. And more taxes and laws will not fix it.

Do we not see that this is divine judgment? 9/11? School shootings? The Middle East? Immorality? Romans 1 gives a precise description of what happens to a nation and an individual when they prefer sin over God.

In our churches, most parishioners are not challenged to invest sacrificially in their giving of their time, talents, and treasures. We have become complacent through the root of convenience.

Compromise prevails and people are flocking to the "Church of No Commitment." Truth is jaded and no one seems to care. O, we say we care but show ourselves hypocrites by being conformed rather than transformed. We're not a peculiar people. You can't tell any difference in us and the world. We see worldly movies, speak worldly words, crave worldly pleasures and our passion is not for Christ.

1 Peter 4:17 says, "For the time has come for judgment to begin at the house of God; and if it begins with us first, what will be the end of those who do not obey the gospel of God?"

Do we care? Do we have an interest in those who do not obey the gospel of God? We say we do. But does it affect our prayer time? Sweet Hour of Prayer has been replaced by open eyed and open ended general statements made in the car on the way to work.

Where is our passion? Where is the urgency? Romans 13:11&12 says, "...knowing the time, that now it is high time to awake out of sleep: for now is our salvation nearer than when we believed. The night is far spent, the day is at hand..."

AMERICA NEEDS REVIVAL!

We who say we are the people of God need to awake out of our sleep. All around us the signs of Christ's second coming prevail.

1. Are you ready? Are you ready for His return?

Paul says in our text "I am now ready to be offered."

You know what being ready is. Ready for work; ready for school; ready for church. Preparation is involved in getting ready. Are you preparing?

The older I get the sooner I tend to be ready. I get places earlier. I get up earlier.

My dear friend Jack Gessells is a victim of ready.

Are you ready? Are you ready to stand before the great "I AM" and give an account of your life? Are you ready for judgment? Are you living a life of transformation rather than conformity?

Are the people you want to be with you in Heaven saved? Are you ready?

2. It won't be long now. The time of our departure through death or rapture will come before you know it. Jesus says we are to always be watching and ready.

I hate aging. Daily, I live in a state of unbelief that I'm 52 years old. It seems like yesterday I was in High School. But life speeds by like a weavers beam. "The harvest is past, the summer is ended, and we are not saved."

Christ is coming. Are you prepared? Do you live in daily anticipation? It won't be long.

3. Are You prepared. Have you fought well? Have you completed the purpose for which God created you? Will you stay true to the end?

Paul sat in that Roman prison with a clear conscience. He was ready. His life would be coming to an end. He had fought well.

And he knew what awaited him: 8 Henceforth there is laid up for me a crown of righteousness, which the Lord, the righteous judge, shall give me at that day: and not to me only, but unto all them also that love his appearing.

You see, Paul knew what Revival was. He had seen it. He participated in it. He contributed to it. And, his purpose fulfilled and his labor ended, he was happy to be going to see his savior, bringing his sheaves with him.

The landscape of our society is very similar to what Paul was accustomed to. He stated passionately in Romans 10, "1 ¶ Brethren, my heart's desire and prayer to God for Israel is, that they might be saved. 2 For I bear them record that they have a zeal of God, but not according to knowledge. 3 For they being ignorant of God's righteousness, and going about to establish their own righteousness, have not submitted themselves unto the righteousness of God."

Are you a Christian? "Christian" is not a label you wear or a tag on a blog but a life you live. As a Christian, you are saying your citizenship resides in eternity and the kingdom of Heaven has your loyalty. Have you been to the cross? Were you transformed by the power of God's Spirit? Are you different than you used to be? If this does not define you, please: be honest with yourself. You are not a Christian – and come to Christ today!

Christian, are you serving your master? Are your passions directed toward Heaven? Are souls being saved because of your witness? Is your heart's desire and prayer for America that they might be saved or are you more concerned about scores and entertainment? Does your church attendance, your giving, your witness, your time, your life, and everything about you reflect that you are HIS?

America is dying. Souls are on their way to Hell. The iceberg has pierced the hull of the ship and she's listing, sinking. Don't go down with this sinking ship. Stand with Paul, Timothy, me, and

Christ and do your part! Let's pray and work to bring this nation to its knees on the altar of repentance because

AMERICA NEEDS REVIVAL!

Now unto him that is able to keep you from falling, and to present you faultless before the presence of his glory with exceeding joy,

To the only wise God our Saviour, be glory and majesty, dominion and power, both now and ever. Amen. (Jude 1:24)

LET US STAND

3
LOVE

Dr. Calvin Evans
Deceased Evangelist and founder of Evangelism Outreach

Love is a little four letter word, but my what a meaning it carries in the Christian life. Many four letter words we hear today carry the wrong meaning and they're invading our language from every side.

Most four letter words receiving attention are words of vulgarity, profanity, blasphemy, or "off color" to say the least. But it seems this four letter word has been almost forgotten by the masses of America today.

Even the language coming from Washington is filled with four letter "expletives." I think this shows us the moral and spiritual sickness in America which is reaching every level of our society. This should concern and challenge every Christian.

Jesus said, when talking about the last days, "Because iniquity shall abound, the love of many shall wax cold" (Matthew 24:12). It's important that we know what the word love really means from the Christian point of view. There are four letters in this word and these letters will form the outline of my message:

I. THE LAW OF LOVE

    O

    V

    E

I think we can say the "L" stands for the law of love. I believe the law of love defines it. Someone has said that it's impossible to define love, that it cannot be explained. It can only be experienced and perhaps this is true.

Love means many things to different people. A young boy who had just fallen in love with his first girlfriend said, "Love is a tickle under the fifth rib."

This is one kind of love, but not what I'm talking about today.

I know a young couple who were married and six weeks later separated and divorced. When asked what happened, they replied, "We just don't love each other anymore." I'm glad God's love for us lasts longer than six weeks. God says in Jeremiah 31:3, "I have loved thee with an everlasting love." Someone has pointed out that if it were possible for us to travel back into the distant past, beyond the time when the first wave had ever beat against the beach, or the first leaf had ever fluttered in the breeze, beyond the time the first star had ever penciled its ray of light across the blackness of this universe, or the first angel had ever worshipped before the throne of God, we would be no nearer the beginning of God's love than we are this present hour.

If we could board the chariot of time and travel into the future beyond time when the moon turns black, the sun grows cold, and the stars fall from heaven, beyond that time when the works of men vanish, and the leaves of God's judgment book shall fall, we would be no nearer the end of God's love than we are at this very moment. Aren't you glad God's love never changes?

We also hear much today about "free love." Love is never free! Genuine love always costs something! "God so loved...He gave" (John 3:16).

God made man in His own image and placed him in Eden. When He did this, He gave man a law to live by. God warned man, that if this law was broken, he would surely die. Man soon broke this law and started down the wide road of destruction, despair, and death. From that moment on, God has always given man a law.

God through Moses, gave man a law to live by. This law said "thou shalt" and "thou shalt not" do thus and so. In our age, God no longer says, "thou shalt" and "thou shalt not," but He simply says, "If a man love me he will keep my words." Romans 13:10 tells us, "Love is the fulfilling of the law."

The law of love is the strongest law in this universe. Love is that motivating force which will cause us to walk uprightly before God. Jesus said, "Thou shalt love the Lord thy God with all thy heart, and with all thy soul, and with all thy mind. This is the first and great commandment. The second is like unto it, thou shalt love thy neighbor as thyself. On these two commandments hang all the law and the prophets"

(Matthew 22:37-40).

The law of love is the balance-wheel of Christianity. Jeb Magruder, a young businessman from California, left his position several months ago to become a special assistant to the President of the United States. May 21, 1974, Jeb Magruder was sentenced to prison for his part in the Watergate affair. During an interview he was asked, "Why did you do it?" He replied, "Somewhere between my ambitions and my ideals, I lost my compass." The law of love is a compass which will give us a sense of direction in the way we should travel.

Robert Oppenheimer, one of the most brilliant minds of this century and the father of the hydrogen bomb, died a middle-aged man. He lived the last fifteen years of his life in seclusion. Before he died, he said to a friend, "I have no purpose in life, I have no scale of values." Thank God, the law of love gives us a scale of values upon which we can build our lives.

L

II. THE OBJECT OF LOVE

V

E

I believe the "O" could stand for the object of love. If the law of love defines it, then we could say the object of love confines it. Love must have an object. If God gave man the law of love to direct his path, then God must also give him an object of love to show him where that path will lead.

Many think of God as an unidentified object of educated vagueness. The Pantheist, for example, teaches that everything is God and God is everything.

They say that God is the air, the trees, the rivers, and the flowers. If this were true, then we could love everything. But it is not true! God is a personal God and He is to be the object of our love.

The Bible teaches that we are to love God and hate the devil. We are to love good and hate evil; love sinners, but hate sin. Jesus says, "No man can serve two masters. For either he will hate the one, and love the other; or else he will hold to the one, and despise the other. Ye cannot serve God and mammon" (Matthew 6:24). A little girl once came to her mother and asked,

"Mother, where is God?" The mother replied, "God is everywhere." But the little girl responded, "I don't want God to be everywhere. I want Him to be somewhere, and I want Him to be someone." How sad is it that many think of God as some vague object whom we can never personally know and love.

Dr. Hyman Appleman tells the story of a wealthy couple who had only one child, a seven-year old daughter. Death took the child from them suddenly. The parents were grief stricken. As soon as the mother had recovered from her initial shock, her friends suggested that she adopt a child. She finally agreed and arrangements were made for her to interview an orphan girl about the same age as her own daughter.

The mother asked to be alone with the little girl. She began to tell the frightened child that she and her husband would like for her to come and live with them. She said, "If you come and live with us, we are rich, and can give you everything you want. You will have a nursery, a pony, and many dolls, along with many other things." The little girl stood there not saying a word. The appeal went on. Finally, the mother was ready to give up in defeat. Then, the little girl looked up in bewilderment and asked, "If I come and be your little girl, and you give me all these things, what do you want me to do?" The mother grabbed that little girl in her arms and said, "All we want you to do is just to love us."

If I know anything about Christianity, the thing God wants most from us, is for us to love Him. God sees man on the road of life with his sins, his frustration, his problems, and says, "If you'll come to me, I'll forgive your sins, cleanse your conscience, fight your battles, be your friend, and finally, give you a home in Heaven." Man looks up and says, "God, if you're going to do all this for me, what do I have to do?" God replies, "I just want you to love me." God did not make us as a puppet on a string. He gave us a mind with which we can know; a heart with which we can feel; and a will with which we can choose. God wants to be that number one object of our love.

We're not only to love God, but also love the brethren. The Bible tells us that one of the evidences of the new birth will be our love for one another. By the way, I believe in the new birth. We must be born again. If we are born again, we'll love the brethren. I John 3:14 says, "We know that we have passed from death unto life, because we love the brethren." The theme of this convention has been Christian growth.

However, there can be no Christian growth without a Christian birth. The reason some people never grow as Christians is because they have never been born again. The baby grows after birth. The sincerity of our love for God will always be reflected in our love for the brethren. "He that loveth not his brother whom he hath seen, how can he love God, whom he hath not seen" (I John 4:20)?

Not only are we to love God, and the brethren, but we are also to love the lost. Jesus teaches us that we are to love one another as He loved us. The world is hungry for a little bit of love. We need to tell the world that Jesus loves them. Jesus had a love and compassion for the lost.

My ministry through radio and television brings me into contact with thousands of people. This makes me keenly aware that there must be millions in America who have no one to love them. Many have grown old. They are shut-in. Their families are gone. If relatives are living, they no longer care. How I pray God will give us the vision and concern we need to try to reach these people and tell them somebody loves them.

L

O

III. THE VIRTUE OF LOVE

E

If the law of love defines it, and the object of love confines it, I think we could say the virtue of love refines it.

I don't know much about refining. I do know, however, it is a process where you take out the impurities. In the thirteenth chapter of First Corinthians, Paul lists many virtues of Christianity, but says the greatest is charity or love. Love is that virtue which lifts Christianity to its highest level of spiritual and moral excellence. Love will meet and conquer every test of life and lift us to a higher level of Christian maturity.

I shall never forget the time when I was saved. I knew I was in sin. I knew I was lost. I didn't know John 3:16 or anything else about the Bible. I didn't have anyone to tell me about the Roman Road but I knew I was lost and my life was a wreck. I came down an aisle and for three days and nights I wrestled with God. (I didn't have to, at least they tell me I didn't have to - but I didn't know that then). I was sick of my life and hungering for something. Finally, when I ceased my struggling and reached up with my little hand of faith and took hold of the nail pierced hand of my Saviour, something happened. When I arose from the altar and looked at that choir, they looked like a convoy of angels God had sent from another world.

The next morning I took a walk up behind the plant where I worked at the time. The sun had never shone as it did that morning! The grass was never as green as it was that morning! The birds had never sung as they did that day! It was the same old world, just a different man.

Somebody said, "He'll never make it over the first weekend." But that has been over 21 years ago. And if I know my own heart, I'm closer to Heaven now than I've ever been in my life.

In this thirteenth chapter, Paul reminds us that it is possible to be a great preacher, a great theologian, a great humanitarian, or even a martyr, but without love, it will profit nothing.

L

O

V

IV. THE EFFECT OF LOVE

If the law of love defines it, the object of love confines it, the virtue of love refines it, then the effect of love outshines it.

D. L. Moody once said, "If I can only convince a man I love him, I can win him." Jesus did not say the world will know you are my disciples because of your greatness, your faith, your works, your name, your fame, or your social status. But Jesus said, "By this shall all men know that ye are my disciples, if ye have love one to another" (John 13:35).

Dr. Herschel Ford tells of a Baptist missionary by the name of Paul Bell, who was a missionary to the Mexicans. One day Paul Bell won an old Mexican woodcutter to Christ. He could not read or write, but he seemed to be gloriously saved. He said, "Brother Bell, I can't read or write. Will you teach me a verse of Scripture and a stanza of a song so I can witness to my people?" Brother Bell taught him John 3:16 and a stanza of that song, "What A Friend We Have In Jesus."

The man promised to come back to church to be baptized. Three weeks passed and he didn't show up. But on the fourth Sunday he came and brought five others with him whom he had led to Christ. The old Mexican woodcutter only lived two years after his conversion, but, during those two years, with only one verse of Scripture and one stanza of a song, he won about fifty others to the Lord. Why? Because he loved his people and wanted to see them saved. Please understand me clearly. I'm not placing a premium on ignorance. What I am saying is, that if we really love God, we can use the capacities and potentials we have and be effective in winning others to Christ. Let's not use our inadequacies and our lack of training as an excuse for not being a soul-winner. One day knowledge will vanish away. One day prophecies shall cease. One day faith will turn into sight and hope will merge into reality, but love will shine on and on. Amen.

4
The Promise of Eternal Life

Mark Price
Pastor Porter FWB church -- Moderator of State Association

In Cleveland, Ohio, there is a sculpted statue called *"Fountain of Eternal Life."* It was designed by Marshall Fredericks, and was dedicated on May 30, 1964 as a tribute to those men and women who had served in World War 2. The sculpture portrays a man escaping the flames of war, reaching heavenward for eternal peace and immortality.

Since the beginning of time, man has always had an unquenchable hunger for immortality.

For instance, in the year 1513, Ponce de León discovered and explored Florida after hearing of the fountain of youth from the people of Puerto Rico. While he was one of the first Europeans to set foot on the American mainland, he never found the fountain of youth.

Then, there is the ancient Japanese fairy tale of the Fountain of Youth. The story goes: *"An old couple lived in the mountains. The man would cut wood, and the woman wove, every day. One day, the man found a spring and drank from it. From drinking, he became a young man. Delighted, he ran home. His wife said that a young man needed a young wife, so she would go and drink. But they should not both be away at the same time, so he should wait. He did wait, but when she did not come back, he went to *look for her. He found a baby by the spring; his wife had drunk too eagerly. Saddened, he carried her back home."*

And who can ignore all of the commercials with journalist, Bill Curtis? In one, Bigfoot is in the background, in another – the Abominable Snowman, in yet another – a leprechaun with his pot of gold. But, my favorite is one in which elderly folks are getting into a pool of water, only to emerge younger. In each of these, Curtis – standing in the foreground - is so proud that "he's discovered the internet." Never mind the deeper earth-shattering discoveries. But, of course, they are nothing more than fable and fiction.

It seems that despite his unquenchable hunger for it, man just always comes up short in his quest for immortality. Of course the reason is simply because he is always looking in all the wrong places.

The rich young ruler knew the proper source. As he ran to Jesus, he asked the timeless question, "What shall I *DO* to inherit eternal life?" You know, people today still make the mistake of asking this question: *"What can we do to possess immortality?"* Each of the Synoptic Gospels records his search.

Of course, we know that the Source is the Son of God, as found in Scripture.

Titus 3:4-7, "But after that the kindness and love of God our Savior toward man appeared, (5) Not by works of righteousness which we have done, but according to his mercy he saved us, by the washing of regeneration, and renewing of the Holy Ghost; (6) Which he shed on us abundantly through Jesus Christ our Savior; (7) That being justified by his grace, we should be made heirs according to the hope of eternal life."

In the KJV, the theme of "Eternal life" appears in Scripture 30 times, and "Everlasting life" appears 15 times.

It is a theme that is woven through all of Scripture.

If you would, turn with me in your Bibles to 1 John, chapter 2.
Let's begin reading together in verse 24, down through verse 28.
"Let that therefore abide in you, which ye have heard from the beginning. If that which ye have heard from the beginning shall remain in you, ye also shall continue in the Son, and in the Father. And this is the promise that he hath promised us, even eternal life, These things have I written unto you concerning them that seduce you. But the anointing which ye have received of him abideth in you, and ye need not that any man teach you: but as the same anointing teacheth you of all things, and is truth, and is no lie, and even as it hath taught you, ye shall abide in him. And now, little children, abide in him; that, when he shall appear, we may have confidence, and not be ashamed before him at his coming." (1 John 2:24-28)

Let "THAT," what? "That which they had heard from the beginning" is the Gospel; the teachings of the Apostles, the original message which had been proclaimed. It had not changed, and would not change.

THEREFORE – We need to ask, "What is the 'therefore' there for?"
In the Greek, it stands emphatically at the beginning of the sentence.
"Ye, therefore, acknowledge the Son, and so shall ye have the Father also." (1 John 2:23)

In vs. 24: John is literally saying, *"But as for you, let that therefore abide in you..."*

ABIDE – "to adhere *steadfastly* to; to allow to obtain a PERMANENT LODGING in your soul; NEVER let it depart from you."

So, John says, *"As for you, let the gospel of Jesus Christ (which you have heard proclaimed from the time you first heard) abide in you forever."* "And," he continues, *"if you will continue in that same gospel, you shall continue in* (abide) *in the Son, and in the Father."*

Vs. 25: *"And this is the promise that he hath promised us, even eternal life."*
(13 words)

Kenneth S. Wuest translates it this way: *"And this is the promise which He Himself promised us, the life, the eternal (life)."*

In our time together, we will consider:
1. The Promise
2. The Source of the Promise
3. The Recipients of the Promise, and
4. The Purpose of the Promise

1. Let us look first at The Promise:
- "The promise" signifies a free promise, given without solicitation
- What does the "promise" contain? *"...the eternal life"* This phrase is so precisely worded that it suggests that there is but one kind of life that forms the sum and the substance of the believer's hope.
- Jesus spoke of it in John 17:2-3: *"As thou hast given him power over all flesh, that he should give eternal life to as many as thou hast given him. And this is life eternal, that they might know thee the only true God, and Jesus Christ, whom thou hast sent."*

"That he should GIVE eternal life..." "Give" suggests a gift. Paul tells us in Romans 6:23, *"For the wages of sin is death, but the GIFT of God is ETERNAL LIFE, through Jesus Christ our Lord."*

Jesus is God's gift to fallen man, that those who believe on Him may be included in the Bride of Christ – the Church.

"... to as many as thou hast given him." The Church is God's gift to Jesus Christ.
- "The Eternal Life" – Life that belongs to God; Life that flows from God, and because it does, it is not affected by the limitations of time.
- *So, we see THE PROMISE...*

2. Secondly, let us consider The Source of the Promise:
- *"And this is the promise that HE hath promised us..."*
- If you or I were to make such a promise, it would be worthless. It would be, because we are incapable of keeping such a promise. No one but the Lord of life could guarantee its fulfillment.
- This is the greatest of all promises given by the greatest of all Promisers.
- For the original readers of John's letter, as well as for us today, we can rest on the promise of eternal life, because of the Promiser Himself – The Source of the Promise.
- *Now, during the time that I was preparing for this message,* there was a question that I struggled with. And that was in regard to who "HE" is referring to in our text (thank Dr. Outlaw, Dr. Reid, Mike Mounts).
- I found evidence such as what Paul wrote to Titus, in Titus 1:2, *"In hope of eternal life, which God, that cannot lie, promised before the world began."*

- This verse, and many like it, indicates that this hope was promised, in Christ Jesus, before the world began, by the Father who is unable to default on His Word.
- For the sake of the context of our text, we will consider the Source of this Promise to be Jesus Christ, the Son of God (see vs. 28, the 'he' and 'him' are clearly referring to Jesus Christ. We are also aware of Jesus' statement, as found in John 10:30, 17:11, and 17:21, "*I and the Father are one.*")
- HE IS ETERNALLY GOD!
    - He was present prior to creation!
    - We are made in His image!
- HE IS TRUTH!
    - He said, "I am the way, the truth and the life; no man cometh to the Father but by me."
- BECAUSE HE IS GOD, and because He is the Truth, He can be trusted to deliver on His promises. He owns the cattle on a thousand hills. It has been added that "He owns the hills and the 'taters (potatoes) beneath those hills." His resources are infinite.

We have considered The Promise, *and* The Source of the Promise.

Now, let us consider...

3. The Recipients of the Promise – US! Very simply, US. (vs. 25)
- US = ALL
- Romans 3:10 - "*As it is written, There is none righteous, no, not one:*"
- Romans 3:23 – "*For all have sinned, and come short of the glory of God;*"
- Romans 5:8 – "*But God commendeth his love toward us, in that, while we were yet sinners, Christ died for us.*"
- John 3:14-18 – "*And as Moses lifted up the serpent in the wilderness, even so must the Son of man be lifted up: (15) That whosoever believeth in him should not perish,*

but have eternal life. (16) For God so loved the world, that he gave his only begotten Son, that whosoever believeth in him should not perish, but have everlasting life. (17) For God sent not his Son into the world to condemn the world; but that the world through him might be saved. (18) He that believeth on him is not condemned: but he that believeth not is condemned already, because he hath not believed in the name of the only begotten Son of God."

WHOSOEVER – US = ALL
- 2 Peter 3:9 = *"The Lord is not slack concerning his promise, as some men count slackness; but is longsuffering to us-ward, not willing that any should perish, but that all should come to repentance."*

ALL!

- John 6:40 – *"And this is the will of him that sent me, that everyone which seeth the Son, and believeth on him, may have everlasting life: and I will raise him up at the last day."*
- US! – The greatest promise, given by the greatest Promiser, is extended to US!
- Okay, we have considered: The Promise, The Source of the Promise, The Recipients of the Promise, finally...

4. The Purpose of the Promise – "... *even eternal life..."*
Q: Do you remember what Jesus said in John 17:3? *"And this is eternal life, that (1) they (US) might know thee the only true God, and (2) and Jesus Christ, whom thou hast sent."*

"That they might know thee..." It is not the amount of knowledge you have, but the *kind* of knowledge that is important. It *is* who you know.

In the same way, it is not the amount of faith you have, but the *kind* of faith that is important. Spurgeon said, *"It is not thy joy in Christ that saves thee. It is Christ. It is not thy faith in Christ, though that be the instrument. It is Christ's blood and merit."* It IS Christ who saves. Life eternal is to know God and to know Jesus Christ. To know Him means to grow in the grace and in the knowledge of Christ.

So, the "promise" is to know the Father and the Son – to abide in them - eternally.

Verse 28 of our text states:
1. We shall have confidence (in what? *His substitutionary and sacrificial death as payment in-full for our sins!*), and
2. We shall not be ashamed at His appearing.

From the foundation of the world, it has been the desire of God's heart to both know and be known by His creation. Mind you, He *knows* every man, woman, boy, and girl.
He *knows* our names, and beyond that, He *knows* the hairs of our heads – He *knows* our DNA!

Jesus gives us a clear definition of *eternal life* in John 17:3; that *we* might know the Father, the "only true God, and Jesus Christ, who the Father has sent."

He desires that we know Him intimately. By the way, that is the very reason that Jesus came – to restore a damaged and deficient relationship between man and God; Emmanuel = "God with us."

Our heavenly Father has gone to the extreme to provide a means through which we can both know Him, and be reconciled to Him. He desires that we walk again with Him in perfect, righteous fellowship just as He walked with Adam and Eve in the Garden, before the fall.

But the Bible is clear that, because of sin, man is spiritually dead and alienated from the life of God. Spiritual and physical death are the result of man's sin. Eternal death in hell is the ultimate penalty for sin. The Scriptures are also clear that it's only through Christ's death that we might live.

For the wages of sin is death ,but the [free] gift of God is eternal life in Christ Jesus our Lord. —Rom. 6:23

He who believes in the Son has everlasting life; and he who does not believe the Son shall not see life, but the wrath of God [presently] abides on him. —John 3:36

And this is the testimony: that God has given us eternal life, and this life is in His Son. He who has the Son has life; he who does not have the Son of God does not have life.
—1 John 5:11-12

I am the way, the truth, and the life. No one comes to the Father except through Me. —John 14:6

Jesus is the very essence of this life. Simply put, Christianity is Christ's life made living in men. If Christ lives in you, then you presently possess eternal life. It's not only a *quantity* of life (regarding the future), more importantly it's also a *quality* of life (regarding the present). It has never been about our merely living forever, but rather our living in complete harmony with a righteous and holy God. Note some of the words that describe this life:

a. It is Eternal life (John. 3:16).
b. It is Abundant life (John 10:10).
c. It is Uncreated life. The very life of God!
d. It is Divine life.
e. It is Resurrection life. The believer has "passed from the realm of spiritual death into the realm of spiritual life" (John. 5:24).

f. It is New life (Rom. 6:4). A newness of quality and character. This new life is characterized by righteousness.

Kenneth Wuest defines and describes this life in this way: The word "life" here is not *bios*, . . ., but *zoe*. This word speaks of life in the sense of one who is possessed of vitality and animation. It is used of the absolute fullness of life, . . . which belongs to God. It is used to designate the life which God gives the believing sinner, a vital, animating, spiritual ethical dynamic which transforms his inner being and as a result, his behavior.

That is the kind of relationship He created us for.

And Adam and Eve had free access to every tree in the Garden, EXCEPT the Tree of Knowledge of Good and Evil. That means that they must have had free access to the Tree of Life, and to experience God's perfect eternal life. But because of their disobedience, they were evicted from the Garden of Eden.

WHY?
Genesis 3:22, "And the Lord God said, "The man has now become like one of us, knowing good and evil. He must not be allowed to reach out his hand and take also from the tree of life and eat, and live forever."

Consider:
Genesis 2:9, 15-17, "And out of the ground made the LORD God to grow every tree that is pleasant to the sight, and good for food; the tree of life also in the midst of the garden, and the tree of knowledge of good and evil... (15) And the LORD God took the man, and put him into the garden of Eden to dress it and to keep it. (16) And the LORD God commanded the man, saying, Of every tree of the garden thou mayest freely eat: (17) But of the tree of the knowledge of good and evil, thou shalt not eat of it: for in the day that thou eatest thereof thou shalt surely die."

And:
Genesis 3:22-24, *"And the LORD God said, Behold, the man is become as one of us, to know good and evil: and now, lest he put forth his hand, and take also of the tree of life, and eat, and live forever: (23) Therefore the LORD God sent him forth from the garden of Eden, to till the ground from whence he was taken. (24) So he drove out the man; and he placed at the east of the garden of Eden Cherubims, and a flaming sword which turned every way, to keep the way of the tree of life."*

By questioning God's Word and authority and twisting His words, the serpent (Satan) initially tempted Eve into eating from the Tree of Knowledge of Good and Evil, an act explicitly forbidden by God. Adam and Eve ate the fruit in rebellion against God's command, despite the warning that *"In the day that you eat of it you shall surely die,"* As a consequence of their sin, Adam and Eve were banished from the Garden of Eden and were denied access to the Tree of Life. Having been separated from the Tree of Life, Adam and Eve became mortal and died, as God had said.

SIN has always kept us from God's best.

Then, in the Book of Revelation, a phrase appears in the Greek three times. This phrase, which literally means *"wood of life"*, is translated in nearly every English Bible version as *"tree of life"* (see Rev. 2:7; and 22:2)

Revelation 2:7 , *"He that hath an ear, let him hear what the Spirit saith unto the churches; To him that overcometh will I give to eat of the tree of life, which is in the midst of the paradise of God."*

Revelation 22:2, *"In the midst of the street of it, and on either side of the river, was there the tree of life, which bare twelve manner of fruits, and yielded her fruit every month: and the leaves of the tree were for the healing of the nations."*

See 1 John 2:27 - "*anointing*" = Holy Spirit...

Look at 1 John 2:28: "*And now, little children, abide in him; that, when he shall appear, we may have confidence, and not be ashamed before him at his coming.*"
(ref. Matthew 25:23, "*His lord said unto him, Well done, good and faithful servant; thou hast been faithful over a few things, I will make thee ruler over many things: enter thou into the joy of thy lord* (eternal life).")

Romans 6:23, "*For the wages of sin is death; BUT, the gift (Promise) of God is eternal life through Jesus Christ our Lord.*"

"*And this is the promise that he hath promised us, even ETERNAL LIFE.*"

John 17:3, "*And this is eternal life, that* (1) *they* (US) *might know thee the only true God, and* (2) *and Jesus Christ, whom thou hast sent.*"
As I close, I want to leave you with this passage and a question: 1 John 5:11-13, "*And this is the record, that God hath given to us eternal life, and this life is in his Son. He that hath the Son hath life: and he that hath not the Son of God hath not life. These things have I written unto you that believe on the name of the Son of God; that ye may know that ye have eternal life, and that ye may believe on the name of the Son of God.*"

The question: **"DO *YOU* KNOW?"**

5

Nevertheless, The Enemy Is Strong
Numbers 13:25-33

Michael J. Gillen, JD
Minister, Attorney, Clerk of Capitol City Conference

In the beginning of Numbers 13, we see a listing of the 12 spies, one from each tribe that were sent to spy out the land of Canaan. These weren't just any men, but we know from verse 2 that they were the rulers of their tribes. In verses 17-20, Moses gives them instructions on how they should spy out the land. In verse 21, the spies started their journey in Kadesh, which was at the northern edge of the wilderness of Paran, which is in modern-day Egypt. They travelled north and a little eastward to Rehob. (v22) Then, they went south and a little eastward to Hebron, which was a low-lying valley area to the hill country (that is why verse 22 says they "ascended to the south" because they were going uphill.) (V23-24) They made it to the brook Eshcol where they cut down a cluster of grapes so large that it had to be carried by two men using a staff in between them. Finally in verse 25 they return to Kadesh.

Numbers 13:25-33

(25) And they returned from searching of the land after forty days.

(26) And they went and came to Moses, and to Aaron, and to all the congregation of the children of Israel, unto the wilderness of Paran, to Kadesh; and brought back word unto them, and unto all the congregation, and shewed them the fruit of the land.

(27) And they told him, and said, We came unto the land whither thou sentest us, and surely it floweth with milk and honey; and this is the fruit of it.

(28) Nevertheless the people be strong that dwell in the land, and the cities are walled, and very great: and moreover we saw the children of Anak there.

(29) The Amalekites dwell in the land of the south: and the Hittites, and the Jebusites, and the Amorites, dwell in the mountains: and the Canaanites dwell by the sea, and by the coast of Jordan.

(30) And Caleb stilled the people before Moses, and said, Let us go up at once, and possess it; for we are well able to overcome it.

(31) But the men that went up with him said, We be not able to go up against the people; for they are stronger than we.

(32) And they brought up an evil report of the land which they had searched unto the children of Israel, saying, The land, through which we have gone to search it, is a land that eateth up the inhabitants thereof; and all the people that we saw in it are men of a great stature.

(33) And there we saw the giants, the sons of Anak, which come of the giants: and we were in our own sight as grasshoppers, and so we were in their sight.

In this message, I want to focus on two things: the report and the enemy.

Before we jump into the spies' report, I want to look quickly on some other verses that talked about the Promised Land.

Deuteronomy 6:22-23 says, "and the LORD shewed signs and wonders, great and sore, upon Egypt, upon Pharaoh, and upon all his household, before our eyes: (23) And he brought us out from thence, that he might bring us in, to give us the land which he sware unto our fathers.

- God's plan when he brought them out of Egypt was to give them the land of Canaan.
- He has the same plan for us today, when he brought you out of the bondage of sin, he did that to bring you in to his will!

The Spies' Report

The Good News

The spies first gave the good news, they showed all of the children of Israel the fruit of the land, the giant cluster of grapes and said that it "floweth with milk and honey."

Exodus 3:8 And I am come down to deliver them out of the hand of the Egyptians, and to bring them up out of that land unto a good land and a large, unto a land flowing with milk and honey; unto the place of the Canaanites, and the Hittites, and the Amorites, and the Perizzites, and the Hivites, and the Jebusites.

1. God had already spied out the land, he knew that the milk and honey were there. Notice that the spies did not bring back any more information than God had already given them.

God wanted them to go up and possess the land but they wanted to send the spies, it was a form of compromise. Just like when Israel later wanted a king and God gave them a king. Moses gave such specific instructions to spy out the land. But God had already told them what the land look like what it was filled with and what people were there. They gained nothing from spying out the land except for fear.

2.   If God lays it on your heart to do something you don't need approval from anyone else, including yourself.

3.   The spies ended up discouraging God's people, then after that they started lying by giving a bad report. The land wasn't filled with quicksand and not everybody was a giant in it. The biggest problem with the spies' report is that they left out God!

Nevertheless

After saying the good news, verse 28 begins with "Nevertheless"

1.   In spite of that, however, yet, despite of that, notwithstanding, although, that said, be as it may, even so, on the other hand, anyhow, nonetheless, but…"the people be strong that dwell in the land, and the cities are walled, and very great: and moreover we saw the children of Anak there."

2.   We use words like "nevertheless" and "but" often, but usually we forget the meaning of them. They are used to lessen or negate everything that comes before them and focus or increase everything that comes afterward.

   a) Have you ever given an apology with the word "but" in it? I'm sorry that I forgot to call you, but I have been so busy.

      1) It lessened the first part (being sorry) and magnified the second part (the excuse).

   b) The way the word is used here shows unbelief. Not only where the 10 spies unbelieving, but all of the children of Israel were convinced with their report. There was an entire nation of unbelief save for a few individuals.

      Hebrews 3:19 "So we see that they could not enter in because of unbelief."

It wasn't the walled cities, and wasn't the Giants that kept them from the Promised Land, it was unbelief!

    c) The worst thing you can do is put a nevertheless after what God has said and promised.

        1) You need to either get rid of it or you can flip the sentence around so that you are lessen the first part and increase the second part. Say that the enemy is strong nevertheless with God all things are possible.

        2) We are in their sight as grasshoppers, nevertheless, Isaiah 40:22 says, "It is he that sitteth upon the circle of the earth, and the inhabitants thereof are as grasshoppers; that stretcheth out the heavens as a curtain, and spreadeth them out as a tent to dwell in:"

3. Even those giants look like grasshoppers to God!

Let me give you an example in the New Testament... Luke 5:4-6 Now when [Jesus] had left speaking, he said unto Simon, Launch out into the deep, and let down your nets for a draught. (5) And Simon answering said unto him, Master, we have toiled all the night, and have taken nothing: nevertheless at thy word I will let down the net. (6) And when they had this done, they inclosed a great multitude of fishes: and their net brake.

    a) God wants faith and obedience. Remember that Peter was an experienced fisherman. And Jesus was asking him to do something that wouldn't have made very much sense to catch fish. Nevertheless he did it and received the blessing.

The Enemy

1. The Amalekites previously attacked the children of Israel unprovoked, when they had just left a period of bondage in Egypt and on top of that, they attacked from behind, where the weaker

and sicker people were. They didn't fight fair. They are a picture of Satan and his attacks.

2. In this passage we see the Amalekites briefly mentioned again. Why? Because the enemy didn't do anything in this story. The Amalekites didn't attack, they didn't threaten, they didn't do anything in this story. We learn from verse 29 that they dwelled in the south, so they would have been the first enemy that the children of Israel would have encountered in taking the Promised Land.

   a) Without lifting a finger or shooting an arrow or riding a chariot, the Amalekites along with the other enemies in the land of Canaan instilled enough fear in the children of Israel that it prevented them from obeying God! The mere existence of the enemy scared them more than the power of God that they had witnessed over and over again!

   b) They were afraid of the Amalekites, but what they needed to do was remember the recipe that worked previously. Exodus 17:11, "When Moses held up his hand, that Israel prevailed."

3. They had already defeated the Amalekites with God's help right after they left Egypt! Why were they worried? God had also defeated the mighty Egyptian army.

   a) Why are you worried about the enemy today? They will be around us all of our lives, but so will God! Don't you remember the last time God defeated the enemy for you?

   b) There may be giants, there may be walled cities with enemies all around, but with God on your side, the victory has already been won!

The Opposing View

1. Caleb was very optimistic about being able to overcome the enemy (v30 - "Let us go up at once, and possess it; for we are well able to overcome it"). But the majority of the children of Israel overcame in fear. This was a very big missed opportunity for the children of God.

   a) The Promise Land had not changed, each and every spy saw the same land, the same blessings, the same benefits and the same enemy. However, the reports are very different, it all depends on your point of view. This same thing happens in board meetings in churches all over the world. God presents the church with a challenge, he promises victory, he wants the church to step out in faith and you have some people that focus on the problem, focus on the enemy, focus on the cost, focus on the sacrifice, but you have others that focus on God and his ability to give us everything that we need in order to do his will!

   b) The children of Israel spent more time spying out the Promised Land than trusting in God. The same is true for us today, we need to spend less time analyzing and measuring the problem, and more time on our knees!

2. The Promised Land always represents Christians living a life of obedience to God and his will. If you decide not to follow God's will for your life even because there are so many around you discouraging you it will be the biggest missed opportunity of your life as well. God never told them to fight the enemy he said go in and possess the land.

6
Reviewing The Present

Alton E. Loveless
Retired Publisher, Pastor, Denominational Executive

Raymond C. Ortlund in his book, LET THE CHURCH BE THE CHURCH, tells of a pilot who announced over his intercom system, "Ladies and gentlemen, I have good news and bad news. The good news in that we have a tailwind and are making excellent time. The bad news is that our compass is broken and we have no idea where we are going."

There is a story in THE LAST HURRAH that illustrates my concern. The mayor of Boston is watching a parade. He says, "There go the people. I am their leader. I must follow them."

Since no one rises higher than leadership takes us, I feel it helpful that we look at the men the Master chose and how He developed leadership. How could Christ take 12 of the most changeable men and move the world. How could Jesus who knows all things make such a mistake in choosing such men of diversity?

May I suggest from the beginning that these were His best friends. And while we are concerned about being his friend we forget these were His whom He had called to train. They, like us, broke His heart many times as He sought to make them leaders.

Most of you probably cannot name all twelve of these men but they appear in the Bible in four different places as an entire group. (Matthew 10:2-5; Mark 3:16-19; Luke 6:14-16; and Acts 1:13).

Matthew 10:2-5
Now the names of the twelve apostles are these; The first, Simon, who is called Peter, and Andrew his brother; James the son of Zebedee, and John his brother; [3] Philip, and Bartholomew; Thomas, and Matthew the publican; James the son of Alphaeus, and Lebbaeus, whose surname was Thaddaeus; [4] Simon the Canaanite, and Judas Iscariot, who also betrayed him. [5] These twelve Jesus sent forth, and commanded them, saying, Go not into the way of the Gentiles, and into any city of the Samaritans enter ye not:

Mark 3:16-19
And Simon he surnamed Peter; [17] And James the son of Zebedee, and John the brother of James; and he surnamed them Boanerges, which is, The sons of thunder: [18] And Andrew, and Philip, and Bartholomew, and Matthew, and Thomas, and James the son of Alphaeus, and Thaddaeus, and Simon the Canaanite, [19] And Judas Iscariot, which also betrayed him: and they went into an house.

Luke 6:14-16
Simon, (whom he also named Peter,) and Andrew his brother, James and John, Philip and Bartholomew, [15] Matthew and Thomas, James the son of Alphaeus, and Simon called Zelotes, [16] And Judas the brother of James, and Judas Iscariot, which also was the traitor.

Acts 1:13
And when they were come in, they went up into an upper room, where abode both Peter, and James, and John, and Andrew, Philip, and Thomas, Bartholomew, and Matthew, James

the son of Alphaeus, and Simon Zelotes, and Judas the brother of James.

Please note that in all four lists in the Bible, Simon Peter is always listed first. Judas always appears last in the lists except in Acts where he has already betrayed the Lord. Note the disciples appear in all four lists in three groups of four. It is interesting to note the same person appears first in each of the three groups. Peter in group one; Phillip in group two; James the Less in group three.

Matthew 10	Mark 3	Luke 6	Acts 1
Simon Peter	Simon Peter	Simon Peter	Simon Peter
Andrew	James	Andrew	James
James	John	James	John
John	Andrew	John	Andrew
Philip	Philip	Philip	Philip
Bartholomew	Bartholomew	Bartholomew	Thomas
Thomas	Matthew	Matthew	Bartholomew
Matthew	Thomas	Thomas	Matthew
James	James	James	James
Thaddaeus	Thaddaeus	Simon	Simon
Simon	Simon	Thaddaeus	Thaddaeus
Judas Iscariot	Judas Iscariot	Judas Iscariot	

They also must have had a partner as well. This is indicated from Mark 6:7 as they were sent out two by two. "And he called unto him the twelve, and began to send them forth by two and two; and gave them power over unclean spirits;"

Sometime in your study observe who ran around with whom.

I believe I can fairly classify these three groups thusly:

Group one:
The Presenters - The Vocal Ones - Authoritarian Leaders
Group two:
The Contenders - The Varied Ones - The Automatic Leaders
Group three:
The Pretenders - The Vacillating One's - Appointed Leaders

Matthew 9:35-10:7, "And Jesus went about all the cities and villages, teaching in their synagogues, and preaching the gospel of the kingdom, and healing every sickness and every disease among the people. But when he saw the multitudes, he was moved with compassion on them, because they fainted, and were scattered abroad, as sheep having no shepherd. Then saith he unto his disciples, The harvest truly is plenteous, but the labourers are few; Pray ye therefore the Lord of the harvest, that he will send forth labourers into his harvest. And when he had called unto him his twelve disciples, he gave them power against unclean spirits, to cast them out, and to heal all manner of sickness and all manner of disease. Now the names of the twelve apostles are these; The first, Simon, who is called Peter, and Andrew his brother; James the Son of Zebedee, and John his brother; Philip, and Bartholomew; Thomas, and Matthew the publican; James the son of Alphaeus, and Lebbaeus, whose surname was Thaddasus; Simon the Canaanite, and Judas Iscariot, who also betrayed him. These twelve Jesus sent forth, and commanded them, saying, Go not into the way of the Gentiles, and into any city of the Samaritans enter ye not; But go rather to the lost sheep of the house of Israel. And as ye go, preach, saying, The kingdom of heaven is at hand."

I. **The Presenters - The Vocal Ones - Authoritarian Leaders**

A. Simon Peter - The Out Front One

1. Tested By Spiritual Inventory

Simon Peter - The task oriented leader. The text called him the first Simon. Not first by order of calling but rather the up-front, out-front man. The Greek word "Protos" is used. The same word is used in I Timothy 4:15, "This is a faithful saying and worthy of all acceptation, that Christ Jesus came into the world to save sinners; of whom I am chief."

Simon Peter. We know more about him than most all the other disciples. Next to the name of Jesus, Peter appears more than any other in the gospels. Nobody speaks as often as Peter and nobody is spoken to by the Lord as often as Peter. He is reproved by the Lord. No one acknowledges the Lordship of Christ as boldly as Peter, yet no one so boldly denied it as Peter.

He has 3 unusual characteristics:

a. **Inquisitive.** Peter asks more questions in the Gospels than all the other disciples combined.

(1) How often should I forgive? (Matthew 18:21).

"Then came Peter to him, and said, Lord, how oft shall my brother sin against me, and I forgive him? Till seven times?"

(2) What reward will we get if we follow? (Matthew 19:27)

"Then answered Peter and said unto him, Behold, we have forsaken all, and followed thee; what shall we have therefore?"

(3) What about the fig tree that has withered? (Mark 11:21).

"And Peter calling to remembrance saith unto him, Master, behold, the fig tree which thou cursedst is withered away."

(4) What about the meaning of the need? (Mark 13:3). "And as he sat upon the Mount of Olives over against the temple, Peter and James and John and Andrew asked him privately,"

b. Initiative. Peter not only asked questions but he was always the one who answered.

(1) When Jesus asked, "Who touched me?" (Luke 8:45) Peter answered.

(2) When Jesus asked, "Who say ye that I am?" (Matthew 16:15-16) Peter answered.

(3) When Jesus asked, "Will you also go away..." (John 6:67) Peter said, "To whom shall we go...you have the word of eternal life."

c. Involved. Leaders are always in the middle of everything.

(1) Matthew 14:29. Peter jumped out of the boat and walked on the water. We criticize him for lack of faith but six others didn't have enough to even jump in.

(2) Peter denied Christ 3 times, but none of the others were nearby. Earlier the men "left all and followed Him" but now they "forsook Him and fled."

(3) After the resurrection, John stood at the entrance of the tomb, but Peter rushed right in.

2. Tainted By Secular Identification

In John 1:42 Jesus at His first meeting of Simon said, "Thou art Simon the son of Jona: Thou shalt be called Cephas, which is by interpretation, a stone."

Simon was the name used when he was referred to by SECULAR identification.

(1) The house of Simon (Mark 1:29).
(2) Simon's wife's mother (Mark 1:30; Luke 4:38).

(3) Simon's boat (Luke 5:3).
(4) Simon's fishing partners (Luke 5:10).
(5) Simon's house (Luke 4:38, Acts 10:17).

When Jesus reprimanded him for SIN he was also called Simon.

(1) Luke 5:4-5, "He said unto Simon, launch out into the deep, and let down your nets for a draught, and Simon answering said unto him, Master, we have toiled all the night, and have taken nothing. Nevertheless at thy word I will let down the net." He is saying, This is ridiculous! We are the professionals. He is just a carpenter, O well. Luke 5:8... "Depart from me; for I am a sinful man, O Lord."

(2) Three times Jesus asked him, "Simon, son of Jonah, lovest thou me?"

(3) When Jesus builds him up, He calls him Peter.

3. Taught By Spiritual Insistence

Vocal leaders often pay dearly. Simon Peter did. You cannot know the impetuous, changeable Simon until you read his two little epistles in the back of the New Testament. Then you will see "The stone."

Vocal leaders would do well to study the life of Simon Peter's inconsistency.

B. Andrew - The Manly One

1. The Testifier Because Of Spiritual Increase

Andrew, whose name means "manly" never broke into the inner circle. Only once is he ever listed with the other three in a group and that is in Mark 13:3 when they sat upon the Mount

Olives and asked Jesus, "Tell us when shall these things be: and what shall be the sign when all these things shall be fulfilled?"

Andrew was never as out front or forward as his brother.

(By the way, how would you always like to be referred to as someone's brother?)

All but one time Andrew is referred to as Simon Peter's brother.) In fact, he is not mentioned in any detail in the first three gospels (his calling, etc.), but in the Gospel of John he is mentioned in three distinct instances and in each he is doing the same thing. He was bringing people to Jesus.

a. John 1:40-42a He brought Peter to Christ.

b. John 6:8-9 He brought the little boy with fish and loaves.

c. John 12:20-22 he brought the Greeks to Christ.

Thank God there dwells among our denomination men still interested in bringing men to Christ. Soul winners who remain unsung and whose churches are growing. However, we need to be careful that our pride of success does not lead us to:

2. A Temptation Due To Satanic Intervention

C.S. Lewis said, "The Source of pride is comparison."

History reveals few great churches exists from times past and they are only a shadow of its greatness. Time is our greatest enemy.

You may have a great church today and you should preach for its very soul for growth. But wait a little while. Give Satan time, your people time, your pride time. But be aware men die, movements fade, monuments fall, and only the message falters not. The flood of Hell cannot prevail upon the church of Jesus Christ.

Our greatest failure is to see things as:

- Physical, not spiritual;
- Earthly, not heavenly;
- As time, not eternal.

We are nearsighted, out of focus;

- Blind to our own conceits;
- Boastful in our own capabilities;
- And burdened by our own carelessness.

We have a tendency to:

- View with human eyes and dim the eye of faith;
- to weigh things on the world's scales, not on eternity's balances;
- and to obscure present realities with pipedreams,
- or fantasies, instead of giving ourselves with courage and faith to changing this world for Christ.

Remember, "History is His story and we have little regard for it."

C. James - The "Hot Head"

1. He Was Temperamental By Implication

James' name always appears before his brother John in the gospels. Perhaps he was the elder or the one of stronger influence. James was a fiery fellow evidence by Luke (9:51-56, "And it came to pass, when the time was come that he should be received up, he steadfastly set his face to go to Jerusalem, And sent messengers before his face: and they went, and entered into a village of the Samaritans, to make ready for him. And they did not receive him, because his face was as though he would go to Jerusalem. And when his disciples James and John saw this, they said, Lord, wilt thou that we command fire to come down from heaven, and consume them, even as Elias did? But he turned, and rebuked them, and said, Ye know not what manner of spirit ye are of. For the Son of man is not come to destroy men's lives, but to save them. And they went to another village.

"Let us pray that fire come from Heaven." I do not believe they would make good missionaries. Do you? Note Jesus rebuked them. In Mark 3:17, Jesus called "...them Boanerges, ---Sons of thunder."

2. His Temporary Message Due To Imprisonment

The only place James appears without John is in Acts 12:1-4 when Herod subdues this zealous, aggressive, passionate, fervent man by taking his head. This occurs only 14 years after he wanted to know on which side of the Lord he would sit in the kingdom.

Acts 12:1-4 "Now about that time Herod the king stretched forth his hands to vex certain of the church. [2] And he killed James the brother of John with the sword. [3] And because he saw it pleased the Jews, he proceeded further to take Peter also. (Then were the days of unleavened bread.) [4] And when he had apprehended him, he put him in prison, and delivered him to four quaternions of soldiers to keep him; intending after Easter to bring him forth to the people."

D. John - The Beloved Disciple

1. The Tantrum Of Indictment

The only time we find John alone in the Gospels is in Mark 9:38 and he is upset. "Master, we saw one casting out devils in thy name, and he followed not us: and we forbade him, because he followeth not us." At this time he was still sectarian, narrow-minded, unbending, and intolerant.

My how we need to work on this. We are a diverse denomination. Born out of it. Still in it! Can't we be diverse without being divisive?

One respondent stated, "Our problem is the vocal minority is unwilling to accept the diversity of our many."

More than half of the replies made mention of our:

- Lack of togetherness
- Division Intolerance of each other
- Lack of brotherly love
- Suspicion and jealousy
- Lack of doctrinal purity

While the other half expressed love and confidence in our leadership and denomination as a whole.

Dr. H. Stephen Shoemake of Louisville, relates a story he picked up. "A Texas rancher bought ten ranches and put them together into one big spread. His friend asked the name of the new ranch. The Texan replied, 'It's called the Circle Q, Rambling Brook, Double Bar, Broken Circle, Crooked Creek, Golden Horseshoe, Lazy B, Bent Arrow, Sleepy T, Triple O Ranch.' 'Wow!' the friend replied, 'I bet you have a lot of cattle.'

'No! Not many survive the branding.'

There is a temptation for us to "brand" each other negatively. But too much branding -- the Texan admitted--can reduce the herd."

- Dear friend if we are to exist, an honest effort of cooperation must prevail at all levels and must be made by every preacher and layperson.

- Defiance and rebellion have no place in the ranks of Godly men. An attitude and spirit of animosity, suspicion, and pride will finally destroy a preacher, person, and place.

- Cooperation enhances unity, to which I am committed.

In Matthew 20:20-24 please note the self-interest of James and John in desiring to sit one on each side of the Lord. Note also they sent their mother to do the job of asking Christ but further find in verse 24 the other ten disciples "Were moved with indignation against the two brethren." "Then came to him the mother of Zebedee's children with her sons, worshipping him, and desiring a certain thing of him. [21] And he said unto her, What wilt thou? She saith unto him, Grant that these my two sons may sit, the one on thy right hand, and the other on the left, in thy kingdom. [22] But Jesus answered and said, Ye know not what ye ask. Are ye able to drink of the cup that I shall drink of, and to be baptized with the baptism that I am baptized with? They say unto him, We are able. [23] And he saith unto them, Ye shall drink indeed of my cup, and be baptized with the baptism that I am baptized with: but to sit on my right hand, and on my left, is not mine to give, but it shall be given to them for whom it is prepared of my Father. [24] And when the ten heard it, they were moved with indignation against the two brethren."

We are at a crossroads and we need to take a lesson from John as we find him becoming the:

2. Truth Presenter From Spiritual Improvement

Two words characterize John's later life and teaching: one is love and the other is witness. He uses the word LOVE more than eighty (80) times and the word WITNESS in some form almost seventy (70) times.

He becomes a real truth seeker. He was also borne out of the same zeal, passion and strength as was his brother James. He, like us had to work on loving his brothers.

One phrase stands out from the mature John. "My little children, love one another."

It is not what you are that is important, but what you are willing to become.

May we learn to:

- Respect the person
- Resist pride
- Restore piety
- Re-examine our priority
- Refine by prayer
- Reform by practice

We come now to:

II. The Contenders - The Varied Ones -- The Automatic Leaders

This type of leader is approachable. One should learn credibility is earned, not demanded.

A. Philip (Means Lover Of Horses)

He was the skeptical, pessimistic, and analytical one. But the Lord uses men like this as

Well. In fact, he is always first in group number two. Our churches and conferences are full of this type person. Men of caution, visionless often, but sometimes it is simply that they want to count the cost.

1. Finding His Potential

The first three gospels don't tell us anything about Philip. But John's gospel mentions him four times.

- **A. John 1:43-46.** Where he is called to follow the Lord and where he leads Nathaniel to Christ.

- **B. John 6:5-7.** Where he was singled out by Christ relative to buying food for the 5,000. His response to Christ was, "We couldn't get 200 pennyworth from the whole crowd." What a shame to respond thusly when Jesus in verse 6 states why, "And this He said to test him; for He knew himself what He would do.

- Philip was a materialist, methodical and mechanical. The type who would take out his pocket calculator and say, "We can't afford it!"

- He appears in the same three chapters as does Andrew but lacks the faith.

- He represents in part our stewardship program. We need to be unified in our denominational giving. We have never taught our people to give Biblically. A host of pastors don't tithe and multitudes of our members have never received the blessings or joy of giving.

- Our churches have been selfish. Therefore, due to the lack of outside giving has resulted in the withholding of God's blessing in every area of our denomination.

- We need a Stewardship Commission to educate us. Or a stronger emphasis in our publications and colleges toward giving beyond our own local church to a total ministry.

- Nearly every strong, virile denomination that is growing today has taught their people the value and blessing of unified giving.

- Out of the top 10 giving states, 6 give through the unified co-op plan. An analyses revealed the fastest growing giving states were in this program. While it does not pay all the bills, those states involved were also the fastest growing toward quotas set by the departments and in e establishing strong state and local agencies.

- In the spirit of fairness however, it should be mentioned that other strong giving states exists who have not adopted this program.

- Have we been against this program because of its author? The argument remains, but those who oppose enjoy spending the benefits none the less.

c. John 12:20-22. Here Philip brings the Greeks that come to him to Andrew who take them to Christ.

d. John 14:8 "Lord show us the Father."

Many men like Philip have walked, led, and sat where Christ is, but have yet to fully see the Father or Son. He followed Christ for over three years, but it is conceivable he represents so many yet today. However, he did have a seeking heart in the midst of his insecurity.

B. Bartholomew (Nathanael)

Only one place tells us anything about him aside from the four lists and that is in John 1:46-51 where he is called Nathanael. Let us note here:

1. The Flaw Because Of Prejudice

He along with Philip, were students of the Scripture as noted in verse 45. But we see his sin when Nathanael was told about Jesus. He said, "Can anything good come out of Nazareth?"

In the recent survey it appeared many were saying, "Can anything good come out of Nashville?"

- On a national level many sense:
- A lack of evangelistic thrust.
- Narrow scope for growth.
- Unwillingness to face the issues.
- Power struggle among departments.
- Leadership out of touch with the pastorate.
- Need new faces in old places.
- Place the Heavenly degree above the Nashville degree.
- Growth department catering just too large churches.

The more complimentary suggestions were:

- Need unity without uniformity.
- Return to Christian love.
- Rekindle the old paths.
- Gear toward the small church to help them.
- Speak to our needs.
- Prepare correspondence courses for leaders-preachers.
- Literature improvement.
- Prepare literature for churches for growth.
- National ministers retreat.
-

Prejudice is an uncalled for generalization based on feelings of superiority.

Prejudice is ugly in any form. It was prejudice that kept the Pharisees from responding because he wasn't from Jerusalem. They said of the apostles in Acts 2:7, 4:13 that they were ignorant, unlearned, Galilean hayseeds. Acts 2:7 "And they were all amazed and marvelled, saying one to another, Behold, are not all these which speak Galileans? " Acts 4:13 "Now when they saw the boldness of Peter and John, and perceived that they were unlearned and ignorant men, they marvelled; and they took knowledge of them, that they had been with Jesus."

Prejudice is used by Satan to blind people.

However, I'm glad Nathanael's prejudice was not deep and we see,

2. His Faith Seen By The Phenomenal One

"Behold an Israelite indeed, in whom is no guile." Verse 47.

Thank God! That while prejudice exists among us, the tribe is dying.

Like, Nathanael our knowledge of the Word is causing us to be less judgmental.

May we be seekers of truth, not bound by prejudice, but honest, open, people of prayer.

Every child of God must one day stand before Christ to have his lifetime of service investigated.

Second Corinthians 5:10 states, "We must all appear before the judgment seat of Christ; that every one may receive the things done in his body, according to that he hath done, whether it be good or bad."

This judgment of believers is exclusively the responsibility of the Lord Jesus Christ. No mere mortal is capable of assuming the place of an omniscient, omnipotent God when it comes to judging men and movements. Finite human beings, regardless of their fundamental pedigree or position, are incapable of looking into another man's heart.

Only God can judge righteously. He said in Jeremiah 17:10, "I the Lord search the heart, I try the reins, even to give every man according to his ways, and according to the fruit of his doings."

This is why the Holy Spirit emphatically declares in Romans 14:4, 10-13: "Who art thou that judgest another man's servant? To his own master he standeth or falleth. Yea, he shall be holden up: for God is able to make him stand...But why dost thou judge thy brother? Or why dost thou set at nought thy brother? For we shall all stand before the judgment seat of Christ. For it is written, As I live, saith the Lord, every knee shall bow to me, and every tongue shall confess to God. So then every one of us shall give account of himself to God. Let us not therefore judge one another anymore: but judge this rather, that no man put a stumbling block or an occasion to fall in his brother's way."

We need to be careful about proclaiming and publishing the latest faults of brethren.

Remarks made against anyone are not worthy to be classified under the heading of 'defending the faith,' but rather as 'sowing discord among brothers,' a sin God adamantly hates (see Proverbs 6:16-19). "These six things doth the Lord hate: yea, seven are an abomination unto him: [17] A proud look, a lying tongue, and hands that shed innocent blood, [18] An heart that deviseth wicked imaginations, feet that be swift in running to mischief, [19] A false witness that speaketh lies, and he that soweth discord among brethren."

Until the Lord is allowed to correct this terrible sin through a Holy Spirit-empowered revival of genuine love, our movement will decline and eventually die.

A healthy body cannot exist without love.

C. Matthew (Levi) - The Worst One

The only picture we see of Matthew is found in three places (Matthew 9:9-13; Mark 2:14-17; Luke 5:27-32).

It is the same incident. That of sitting at the seat of custom. Note:

1. The Fame From Which He Propels

He was a tax collector. However, he was willing to leave it entirely. Being a publican was not easy. It was even worse when you know the scriptures of y our fathers but not permitted in the temple because you were a Publican. There were outcast. Remember the publican who sat afar off and said, "God be merciful to me a sinner."

The Jewish Talmud said, "It is righteous to lie and steal from tax collectors."

Matthew must have felt he was the worst one of the lot because he alone in the listings of the twelve gives his occupation as a publican. The publicans were hated and despised by the Jewish society.

Matthew in recording this is showing his genuine humility and expressing his sinful unworthiness.

While Matthew never speaks, never asks a question, never appears in another incident, his book is loaded with an appreciation for Christ.

2. The Forgiveness He Proposes

Matthew 9:9-13, "And as Jesus passed forth from thence, he saw a man, named Matthew, sitting at the receipt of custom: and he saith unto him, Follow me. And he arose, and followed him. And it came to pass, as Jesus sat at meat in the house, behold, many publicans and sinners came and sat down with him and his disciples. And when the Pharisees saw it, they said unto his disciples, Why eateth your Master with publicans and sinners? But when Jesus heard that, he said unto them, they that be whole need not a physician, but they that are sick. But go ye and learn what that meaneth, I will have mercy, and not sacrifice: for I am not come to call the righteous, but sinners to repentance."

The theme of Matthew's message can in part be summed up in this same chapter as he asks which is greater, "to be saved from your sins or healed."

This book, called the Book of the King of Kings to the Jews, perhaps is so noted due to his including more Old Testament quotes of the Law and History than all the other gospels combined.

May I draw your attention to the distance he comes in order to follow Christ.

There were two classes of Tax collectors: The Gabbai and Mokhes.

The Gabbai were the general collectors that collected property tax, income, poll tax, etc.

The Mokhes collected duty and tolls on everything. They were divided into two groups. The Great Mokhes who hired others to do the collecting as he faded from sight and the little Mokhes who were too greedy to hire anyone else.

Matthew is saying I was a little Mokhes. I came from the table. I was saved from the undermost to the uttermost.

He like another publican (Zacchaeus) did something no one else did after their conversion. They gave a banquet for their Savior.

D. Thomas - Not A Doubter

What do you think of when you think of Thomas? Doubter? If you do you believe wrong. I believe he got bad press. Let us look at:

1. His Faith We Desire To Reprove

In John 10:39 we find the account of where Jesus and the disciples had left Jerusalem because of the plot to take his life. But in John 11:14-16 the news of Lazarus's death is received and Jesus decides to return back to Bethany near Jerusalem. This caused a panic by the disciples except Thomas.

"Let us also go, that we may die with him." Verse 16b.

This is not characteristic of doubters but rather because he totally believed in Christ.

John 14:1-5 "Let not your heart be troubled: ye believe in God, believe also in me. In my Father's house are many mansions: if it were not so, I would have told you. And if I go and prepare a place for you, I will come again, and receive you **unto** myself; that where I am, there ye may be also. And whither I go ye know, and the way ye know. Thomas saith unto him, Lord, we know not whither thou goest; and how can we know the way?" Here he is saying, Lord don't you go somewhere we can't come. Thomas had a problem with separation. I don't like what I hear. You are going somewhere and we can't get there. We'll never find the place.

Jesus was crucified in John 19 and Thomas was destroyed. In John 20:24-29 we have the account of the disciples being gathered in the upper room after the crucifixion but Thomas was not there.

I knew it! He died and I didn't. I wanted to go with him and be where he is but he is gone.

He was depressed and had left the others who by the way were in the upper room "for fear."

Thomas was probably kicking every can in Jerusalem. He believed He was gone.

Before you label Thomas "the doubter" remember that none of the other disciples believed

Jesus had risen until they saw him.

We should see Thomas in the light of John 20:29, "Thou hast believed." Here we see:

2. His Fidelity We Should Reduplicate

Our faith and trust falters and our denomination needs to return to a stronger and deeper commitment to the Christ of our salvation.

We must take a look at our faith in what He wants to do in and through us.

We need to:
    a. Define our Purpose - that's Motive.
    b. Discover our Potential - that's Measure.
    c. Determine our Priorities - that's Manner.
    d. Direct our Program - that's Message.

Remember the Lord builds His church with:
    a. A Sanctified Preacher.
    b. A Separated People.
    c. A Salvaging Passion.
    d. A Saturating Program.

I am a denominational person owing my conversion to this movement, but frankly I'm not sure God is a thrilled that there is a Free Will Baptist denomination as I am. But, I am sure he is concerned about my indifference to the lost or my lack of reaching the lost here and around the world.

He is more concerned that people are saved than we continue as a denomination.

The reason any organization exists is to fulfill its preamble. If it wavers it has lost its reason to be. The responsibility is ours. We may:

      a. Shirk it, because we are afraid to undertake it.
      b. Shelve it, because we are anxious to defer it.
      c. Shed it, because we are tired of hearing it.

Or,

      a. Shoulder it, because we are ready to fulfill it.
      b. Share it, and be wise in distributing it.

Men or every level who are known as leaders but whose pride robs of true repentance can create a dike holding back the needful revival for themselves and those they influence.

The streams of revival are held back when cold hearts continue to hold ill feelings. We will never experience revival and restitution:

    a. Until pastors and parishioners forgive each other.
    b. Until churches and conference forgive each other.
    c. Until states and leaders forgive each other.
    d. Until every organization can say, I forgive!

When all our people: from President to pastor; leader to layman; can practice Matthew 18:15. "Moreover if thy brother shall trespass against thee, go and tell him his fault between thee and him alone: if he shall hear thee, thou hast gained thy brother."

Then and only then will we move forward. Until we do, one must surely be fearful in saying, "let us go that we may die with him." How can He forgive us our trespasses when we don't. May the fountains of the Water of life, the Washing of regeneration once again flow and flood every member of our denomination.

III. The Pretenders -- The Vacillating One's -- Appointed Leaders

This third group represents a segment of our movement and they are many.

In many ways our people are suffering from a lack of good leadership. A vast number of our membership have a mistrust of denominational affiliation due to misinformation. Communication falls rapidly from the National to the local church.

A great transition exists today with a stronger emphasis being given to the local and state ministries. In fact, 22 states now have their own State Executive or Promotional Secretaries where the state and national programs are being promoted and with time a stronger program from the local conference to national convention will exit. National Organizations would better their own programs by coordinating with these state leaders.

We now have 28 regular state conventions, 17 Free Will Baptist Bible Institutes in 10 states, 75 Christian schools in 22 states, 13 or so full-time evangelists, 4 colleges geographically centered across the United States, 9 National Boards and Commissions made up of 68 men and women, with 110 Foreign missionaries in 9 countries and 122 Home missionaries in 28 states and Canada, Mexico, Virgin Islands, and Puerto Rico. We also have 8 chaplains serving in the Armed services. In addition the National Sunday School Department dedicated a new Spanish curriculum this year adding to its 1 million, 400 thousand yearly units of printed curriculum.

Our statistics reveals we have 210 district associations, 2,598 churches and 213,025 members.

With plenty of prayer, preparation and a positive approach we can reach into every area of our denomination like never before.

Now let us look at these four disciples who always appear in this group. Just like our mass of people of whom we know so little, these disciples are the ones of whom we know only a little.

A. James - The Son Of Alphasus

The only thing the Bible tells us about this disciple is his name. He never says a word nor is spoken to, but he is still one of the twelve.

1. The Designation His Name Presents

In Mark 15:40 he is called "James the Less." The Greek word used in this title is "mikros" which means little. However, while it basically means "small in stature."

Could it also mean "young in age" or "one of little influence?"

We may never know, but the Bible does tell us.

2. Some Details Of His Pedigree

a. Could Matthew have been his brother?

According to Mark 2:14 Levi (Matthew) was also a son of Alphasus.

b. Could Jesus be his cousin?

In John 19:25, "Now there stood by the cross of Jesus His mother, and His mother's sister, Mary the wife of Clopas..."

Can we assume that no mother would name two daughters Mary and that she was actually a sister-in-law of Mary? Also, Clopas is another form of the name Alphasus. Is it possible that Alphasus as Joseph's brother making Christ and James cousins? To further substantiate this is Mark 15:40 where it refers to a Mary as "The mother of James the Less."

This James represents a vast multitude of our movement. There are thousands of people, mainly in leadership roles in churches and conferences, totally unknown outside his area. He is none the less their leader, and his influence, while little nationally or statewide, is followed locally. He is the overlooked person and is the person to be reached before the grassroots will ever be touched.

Be as it may, while not recognized outside his region, he like James will be recognized in Heaven. The Lord does use obscure, little, unknown, unsung men.

B. Lebbaeus (Judas Thaddaeus)

1. The Definition Of His Personality

His name was Judas (Jehovah leads).

The names Lebbaeus and Thaddaeus may have been added at a later time to reflect his character.

Thaddeus comes from the Hebrew root Thad. It carries with it the meaning of being a "breast-child." He may have been the youngest child. The baby of the family.

Lebbaeus comes from the Hebrew root Lab, which means "heart." A man of courage -- a heart-child.

2. The Declaration Of His Priorities

This man was also lost in obscurity but we find him one time in the scripture.

John 14:21-24, "He that hath my commandments, and kept them, he it is that loved will manifest myself to him. Judas smith unto him, not Iscariot, Lord, how is it that thou wilt manifest thyself unto us, and not unto the world? Jesus answered and said unto him, If a man love me, he will keep my words: and my Father will love him, and we will come unto him, and make our abode with him. He that loveth me not keepeth not my sayings: and the word which ye hear is not mine, but the Father's which sent me."

Jesus' answer simply put would be, "I can tell who loves me by the way they obey me. And only those who truly love **me** and obey me will I manifest myself to. The only people who will be able to perceive me are the ones who love me."

In other words, manifestation is limited to reception.

I believe ones dedication will be determined by:

    a. The Master you serve.

    b. The Message you share.

c. The Morals you sanction.

d. The Manners you show.

It was Bob Jones, Sr. who said, "The level of Responsibility is determined by the level of opportunity."

- A leadership with integrity does not wait to see what the trends are, or what is popular.
- The true leader sets the trends and rallies the people, even when the cause is unpopular.
- How can the church remain silent when millions of unborn infants are being slaughtered?
- How can the church remain silent when we are having an epidemic of divorce and are witnessing the breakdown of the family?
- How can the church remain silent when racism has become sophisticated and hidden in political philosophy?
- How can the church remain silent when there are those who are demanding that homosexuality be recognized as a valid Christian life style?
- How can the church remain silent when our culture is drowning in a sea of alcohol? Where are the Carry Nations of our time?

C. Simon -- The Zealot (Jealous For The Law)

In Matthew and Mark, Simon is identified as "Simon the Canaanite."

Luke and Acts record him as "Simon, called Zelotes." The Greek word used for Zelotes has the same meaning as the Hebrew root quana where the transliteration Kananaios is used.

The meaning of the words being "to be jealous."

Simon may have been identified with a party of Judaism known as the Zealots. His was one of the four dominant groups within Judaism! The Pharisees, Sadducees, Essenes, and the Zealots.

1. The Doctrine He Presented

The zealots were the most fervent, passionate, patriots of Judaism. Probably born out of the Maccabean period where Judas Maccabaeus led a revolt against Greek influences on the Jewish nation and religion. The intensity of the Zealot philosophy is seen in I Maccabees 2:50, "Be ye zealous for the law and give your lives for the covenant."

In New Testament times the Zealots fled to Massada after the destruction of Jerusalem led by a man named Eleazar. Here 960 zealots committed suicide rather than be taken by the hated Roman enemy according to Josephus, the Jewish historian (Wars of the Jews, book VII, Chapters VIII and IX).

2. His Determination Above His Partner

I believe that Simon's partner was Judas Iscariot as Jesus sent out the disciples two by two (Mark 6:7).

But Simon continued to believe and was transformed. Judas however fell short of the Mark.

I believe as Free Will Baptists we have failed to indoctrinate our people. We give up more people to denominations with a foreign biblical doctrine than we receive from others. I have observed many people join our churches across our denomination as I visit churches. Many were made members without having knowledge of our beliefs. Most didn't have the opportunity to even reject our covenant because it wasn't read to them. Many will never be taught our doctrine. That which made us what we are was a common belief and an abiding conviction about apostasy, feet washing, free communion, and local church autonomy separating us from other denominations and their beliefs. These beliefs have been the chains that bind us together.

Many movements that are growing today are not side stepping doctrinal emphasis, but make it the center of their preaching along with salvation. The stress is on conversion, baptism, joining the local church, and living separated lives. Until we do this our losses will continue.

D. Judas Iscariot

The name Judas was a common one. Simply the Greek from of Judah-the land of God's people. Some say its root meaning is "Jehovah praised" but others "one who is the object of praise."

In any case it is sad that it was given to the one who rejects his Lord.

Iscariot basically comes from a combination of the Hebrew term Ish, which means "man," and Kerioth, the name of a town. He was the "Man of Kerioth." He was Judas of Kerioth.

In fact, he was the only disciple not from Galilee since Kerioth was in Judea near Hebron south of Jerusalem. Since he was not one of the acquaintances or brothers could it be he was never accepted as one of the group? However, he continues even from the beginning.

Remember Jesus demanded total commitment as early as John 6:66, "From that time many of His disciples sent back, and walked no more with him." Many left but the twelve stayed. Could he have been motivated by selfish purposes? What type of relationship did he have with Christ?

Psalm 41:9, "Yea, mine own familiar friend in whom I trusted who did eat of my bread, hath lifted up his heel against me."

Psalm 55:12-14, 20b-21, "For it was not an enemy that reproached me; then I could have born it. Neither was it he that hated me that did magnify himself against me; then I would have hid myself from him: But it was thou, a man mine equal, my guide, and mine acquaintance. We took sweet counsel together, and walked unto the house of God in company...............he hath broken his covenant. The words of his mouth were smoother than butter, but war was in his heart: his words were softer than oil, yet were they drawn swords."

Zechariah 11:12-13, "And I said unto them, if ye think good, give me my price; and if not, forbear. So they weighed for my price thirty pieces of silver. And the Lord said unto me, cast it unto the potter: a goodly price that I was prised at of them. And I took the thirty pieces of silver, and cast them to the potter in the house of the Lord."

John 17:12, "While I was with them in the world, I kept them in thy name: those that thou gavest me I have kept, and one of them is lost, but the son of perdition; that the scripture might be fulfilled."

Luke 22:21-22, "But behold, the hand of him that betrayed me is with me on the table. And truly the Son of man goeth, as it was determined: but woe unto that man by whom he is betrayed!"

1. His Desires During The Pretense

Judas never has a word to say until he complains about the money that Mary wasted in anointing Jesus' feet. This is the first time he speaks in the entire biblical record.

John 12:3-6, "Then took Mary a pound of ointment of spikenard, very costly, and anointed the feet of Jesus, and wiped his feet with her hair: and the house was filled with the odour of the ointment. Then saith one of his disciples, Judas Iscariot, Simon's son, which should betray him, Why was not this ointment sold for three hundred pence, and given to the poor? This he said, not that he cared for the poor; but because he was a thief, and had the bag, and bare what was put therein."

Remember The Same Sun That Melts The Wax Hardens The Clay.

Was he the hypocrite of hypocrites? No one even suspected him. Outwardly, Judas appeared not to have a defective character. In fact, he was not even considered a betrayer right up to the last supper by his peers. When he left the upper room the other disciples thought he had only gone out to buy more food.

Judas had heard the same lessons as the other disciples.

    a. The unjust steward (Luke 16:11-13).
    b. The wedding garment (Matthew 22:11-14).
    c. Lessons about money (Matthew 23:1-12).
    d. Jesus even forewarned by saying in John 6:70b, "One of you is a devil." Even John 13:21, "Verily, verily, I say unto you that one of you shall betray me."

2. The Distance He Planned

John 13:10b-11, 18-19, 21-29, "He that is washed need not save to wash his feet, but is clean every whit: and ye are clean, but not all. For he knew who should betray him; therefore said he, ye are not all clean.....I speak not of you all: I know whom I have chosen: but that the scripture may be fulfilled, he that eateth bread with me hath lifted up his heel against me. Now I tell you before it come, that, when it is come to pass, ye may believe that I am he.....When Jesus had thus said, he was troubled in spirit, and testified, and said, Verily, verily, I say unto you , that one of you shall betray me. Then the disciples looked one on another, doubting of whom he spake. Now there was leaning on Jesus' bosom one of his disciples, whom Jesus loved. Simon Peter therefore beckoned to him, that he should ask who it should be of whom he spake. He then lying on Jesus' breast saith unto him, Lord, who is it? Jesus answered, He it is, to whom I shall give a sop, when I have dipped it. And when he had dipped the sop, he gave it to Judas Iscariot, the son of Simon. And after the sop Satan entered into him. Then said Jesus unto him, that thou doest, do quickly. Now no man at the table knew for what intent he spake this unto him. For some of them thought, because Judas had the bag, that Jesus had said unto him, buy those things that we have need of against the feast; or, that he should give something to the poor."

Matthew 26:16, "And from that time he sought opportunity to betray him."

Mark 14:11, "And when they heard it, they were glad, and promised to give him money. And he sought how he might conveniently betray him."

Luke 22:6, "And he promised, and sought opportunity to betray him unto them in the absence of the multitude."

John 18:2-4, "And Judas also, which betrayed him, knew the place: for Jesus ofttimes resorted thither with his disciples. Judas then, having received a band of men and officers from the chief priests and Pharisees, cometh thither with lanterns and torches and weapons. Jesus therefore, knowing all things that should come upon him, went forth, and said unto them, whom seek ye?"

Matthew 27:3,5, "Then Judas, which had betrayed him, when he saw that he was condemned, repented himself, and brought again the thirty pieces of silver to the chief priests and elders. And he cast down the pieces of silver in the temple, and departed, and sent and hanged himself."

Acts 1:18, "Now this man purchased a field with the reward of iniquity; and falling headlong, he burst asunder in the midst, and all his bowels gushed out."

Matthew 27:6-7, "And the chief priests took the silver pieces, and said, it is not lawful for to put them into the treasury, because it is the price of blood. And they took counsel, and bought with them the potter's field, to bury strangers in."

Acts 1:15-26, "And in those days Peter stood up in the midst of the disciples, and said, (the number of names together were about an hundred and twenty.) Men and brethren, this scripture must needs have been fulfilled, which the Holy Ghost by the mouth of David spake before concerning Judas, which was guide to them that took Jesus. For he was numbered with us, and had obtained part of this ministry. Now this man purchased a field with the reward of iniquity; and falling headlong, he burst asunder in the midst, and all his bowels gushed out. And it was known unto all the dwellers at Jerusalem; insomuch as that field is called in their proper tongue, Aceldama, that is to say, the field of blood. For it is written in the book of Psalms, Let his habitation be desolate, and let no man dwell therein: and his bishoprick let another take. Wherefore of these men which have companied with us all the time that the Lord Jesus went in and out among us. Beginning from the baptism of John unto that same day that he was taken up from us, must one be ordained to be a witness with us of his resurrection. And they appointed two, Joseph called Barsabas, who was surnamed Justus, and Matthias. And they prayed, and said, Thou, Lord, which knowest the hearts of all men, shew whether of these two thou hast chosen. That he may take part of this ministry and apostleship, from which Judas by transgression fell, that he might go to his own place. And they gave forth their lots; and the lot fell upon Matthias; and he was numbered with the eleven apostles."

Psalms 69:25-28, "Let their habitation be desolate; and let thy wrathful anger take hold of them. Let their habitation be desolate; and let none dwell in their tents. For they persecute him who thou hast smitten; and they talk to the grief of those whom thou hast wounded. Add iniquity unto their iniquity: and let them not come into thy righteousness. Let them be blotted out of the book of the living, and not be written with the righteous."

Judas represents those of our movement falling short of God's purpose for his life.

Today we have a faltering family unit, pastors and laymen alike are falling speedily into the separation of the family. Many of our great and good men, preachers of the gospel, have become victims of divorce.

Others are open prey for Satan's attack. It is advisable to remember Philip Brooks saying, "If God called you to preach, never stoop to be a king."

We need like never before a Family Life Commission and a strong emphasis on the Christian family in every area of our movement. It cannot be left to the clergy for they are hurting to and the church needs the message

Conclusion

Teaching our people is one of our failings. Another is legalism. We seem to have the idea no better way exists than our own. With this type of attitude, our churches will cease to meet the needs of a changing society. I think most of our churches have reached the height of their growth. I don't think it's impossible for them to grow; I think it's improbable that they will. Therefore, if our denomination is to grow it will take new churches being organized. It will take men dedicated to the cause of growing a church for the cause of Christ.

Since there is a constant upward mobility involved in society as a whole, we need to strengthen, maintain, nourish, and develop our existing churches. We must open new churches for our children who are leaving our rural areas and going to cities, graduating from universities, becoming involved in industry. We cannot forget to serve every area of our changing society. The district conference must band together and train and help our new or young minister to begin churches in areas not reached.

On a national level, we need to capitalize on what God had allowed us to have as denominational resources--our Bible College, Sunday school department, executive office, and mission departments. These departments are not mini-denominations with only their desire in mind. But we are one denomination with many organizations that need to remember we are one.

Our colleges need to produce men who are dedicated to our cause who believe we are a total denomination without prejudice to the uneducated or Non-bible College trained minister. Our mission departments should gear up in fulfilling the design of their organization with a cooperating spirit as the body advances. Our publications should foster unity in the body, and our curriculum press prepare material designed for edification

All working together will provide the impetus we need for a unity which will produce growth.

The first Austrian to ever win a gold medal did so in the 1968 Olympics with a hand gun. He hit the bull's eye 100 times for a perfect score. Upon his return to Austria he was highly honored by his countrymen and sent out to inspire the youth. After the fanfare died he returned to his job. Only a short time later he lost his left hand in the machine at the plant he worked.

Remembering the past he became quite discouraged. In fact, very hard to live with. One evening he came in pushing aside his wife and entered the bedroom where in the chest he found a pistol. His wife, knowing his deep despair, fell to her knees, paralyzed as she cried, "Oh, no." From the home he left crossing over the hillside. SHE SUDDENLY HEARD A BANG. Jumping to her feet she hastened and just as she hastened to the sound, just as she peered over the hillside, suddenly another bang. bang. bang. bang.

In 1972 he won his second gold medal by hitting the bull's eye 99 out of 100 times.

He, while discouraged and despaired and crippled faltered, never lost his dream.

7
The Discovery Of Authority
Matthew 14:22-30

Shawn Beauchamp
Pastor Canaanland FWB church -- Grove City

What is interesting about this placement….is….. This story is immediately following the feeding of the 5,000. It is not coincidence….I believe it is to remind us that often times after the last miracle God wants us to leave that place and miracle….in order to see a greater miracle that lays just ahead!

In spite of all of the wonderful things God has already done…..He pushes us forward in order that we do not miss even better things He has ahead of us!

You have to part with the last in order to get the next!!!!

You know the story….He goes alone to pray and sends them out into the storm….knowing what they are about to face. He knows they are going to run into a severe storm….YES, A VICTORY TOOK PLACE WHEN THEY FED THE 5,000 BUT A GREATER VICTORY AWAITS AHEAD. This sending us into storms….is done by Jesus Himself I also believe to make sure we understand that those who preach a Gospel that says in order for you to be in a storm…you must be out of the Will of God!!!!

But when your theology is Biblical…every trial or difficulty is not necessarily because you are out of the will of God ---…..there is a lesson to be learned in the storm.

One thing that is absolutely clear when we read the Bible...you will see that Jesus has ALL POWER

It must be very clear that in Scripture....when you read about Jesus ....He is pictured as having ALL POWER OVER ALL THINGS.....JESUS HAS ALL POWER & HE HAS ALL POWER OVER ALL THINGS

IN FACT JESUS SAID OF HIMSELF IN

Matthew 28:18....all power is given unto me in heaven and in earth.

When you study the Synoptic Gospels...& YOU READ THE WONDERFUL BOOK OF JOHN....Jesus' power is displayed in many different ways...POWER OVER DEMONS, DISEASE, DISTRESS, AND POWER OVER DEATH!!!!!

I specifically mention these areas...because any and every problems that you walked through the door this morning with....will fit in one of these categories!!!!!

No matter what we confront or face....we must understand....whatever it is...JESUS CHRIST HAS POWER OVER IT....THIS POWER I speak of this morning.....IS A CONQUERING POWER....This Power made violent seas ---still, this Power made the sick --- healed, this power made the dead come to life.

UNDERSTAND: There were many who may have denied His claims, but honey...no one could deny His power

I want to make the case today....that we can walk IN DOMINION.

There is no reason to feel defeated---To constantly walk floors of nervousness—To run from problems....

GOD THROUGH HIS SON JESUS CHRIST HAS GIVEN US AUTHORITY!!!!!

THIS TEXT IS SPECIAL BECAUSE THIS TEXT DISPLAYS…..HIS AUTHORITY!

Peter started walking on the water….vs. 24 the boat was battered by the waves….and the winds were blowing against them….but amid that condition….vs. 29 says….Peter got out of the boat…the boat that was battered by the waves and blown around by the wind…..

HE DID NOT WAIT FOR THE WAVES TO STOP BASHING & THE WIND TO STOP BLOWING….AMID THIS TURMOIL…….HE SAW JESUS AND HEADED FOR HIM!!!!

HE GETS OUT OF THE BOAT & STARTS WALKING ON THE WATER….I WANT TO EMPHASIZE THAT because ….when you are walking towards Jesus….everything isn't going to be smooth!!!!!

GOD CAN PUT YOU IN A SCENARIO WHERE EVERYONE WOULDN'T BE SUCCESSFUL & the circumstances might NOT BE A PERFECT ATMOSPHERE…..BUT YOU HAVE SO MUCH OF GOD IN YOU & ON YOU….THAT YOU CAN STILL MAKE PROGRESS….and there are many here today that can say….despite situations where many would have waved the white flag of surrender---or thrown in the towel a long time ago…..YOU CAN MAKE IT & GET TO WHERE GOD WANTS YOU TO GO!!!!!

THAT IS GOOD NEWS…..BECAUSE WHEN GOD EMPOWERS YOU…YOU CAN THRIVE IN CONDITIONS ……THAT OTHERS COULDN'T

Look @ this disciple that later denies Jesus—HE DOES THE MOST UNTHINKABLE THING I HAVE EVER SEEN!!!!!!....He has enough faith to WALK ON SOMETHING THAT WAS DESIGNED TO MAKE HIM SINK

But the truth is….most people are Comfortable in the boat!!! In their Comfort zones!!!

Most people would rather stay in the boat...rather than getting their feet wet!!!

REAL FAITH IS WHEN YOU LEAVE THE NATURAL OR KNOWN...& DO THINGS YOU NORMALLY ARENT ABLE TO DO!!!!!!

WHEN YOU TRUST GOD & KNOW HE HAS ALL AUTHORITY

1.   We see THE SOVEREIGNTY OF CHRIST

If you are going to have the Authority of God.....you have to see Christ OVER every situation.

The disciples here can only see the STORM......ITS STRENGTH....IT POSSIBILITY TO BRING THEM DOWN!!!!

The Bible tells us in vs.24-25....the disciples are up against the 3 w's...the WAVES---the WIND--- the fourth WATCH of the night.

- THE Waves were frightening
- THE Winds were forceful
- & the Watch was the 4th...meaning

This is the kind of environment or situation where people do not NORMALLY have ANY SUCCESS!!!!

MEANING: a situation where one does not have a chance to SUCCEED OR HAVE ANY AUTHORITY!!!!

THE BIBLE SAYS....IN VS. 25----JESUS COMES TO THEM WALKING ON THE WATER... ....THE WATER WAS THE PROBLEM---YET, JESUS...IS WALKING ON THE WATER....

- The reason why they are scared ....
- The reason they are afraid...
- The reason they are upset....

Is because the waves are beating against the boat...& here comes Jesus....walking on the PROBLEM!!!!

I GET HAPPY HERE... --That which is over there head...is still UNDER HIS FEET!!!!

The reason you can get happy if you know Jesus today....is because no matter what is swirling around you and threatening to take you under........JESUS CAN WALK ON TOP OF ALL OF IT!!!!!

What the disciples do is....they literally see The Sovereign God over their situation....as big & bad as the waves seem to be....JESUS IS BIGGER.....as forceful as the winds may be......JESUS IS BIGGER ----YOU MAY THINK YOU HAVE A BIG PROBLEM.....BUT I AM HERE TO TELL YOU....THE LORD TODAY IS STILL LARGER THAN THE PROBLEM!!!!!

NOW, I DON'T KNOW WHAT PROBLEMS YOU HAVE TODAY....

- I don't know what mountains seems to high today
- I don't know what storm seems so dark and dangerous and insurmountable.......

IT IS ALL STILL UNDER HIS FEET......AND SINCE IT IS UNDER HIS FEET....YOU CAN SURVIVE.....BUT YOU HAVE TO SEE THE SOVEREIGN OVER THE SITUATION

What is great to me personally about vs. 25 is....the text teaches us that this storm that these disciples are in ....IS FIERCE & JESUS COMES TO THEM!!!!!

The parallel scriptures that involve this story say this about the incident......John 6:19 suggests that they are tired---Mark 6:48 suggests they are toiling-----Matthew 14:24 suggests that they are being tossed....the verses we read tells us that they were in something....WATCH THIS NOW.....THAT THEY CANNOT GET OUT OF THE STORM!

BUT UNDERSTAND.....THIS........The storm is too strong for them to get to Him.....but the storm is not so strong that Christ can't get to them!!!!

That tells me...that whenever I am in something that makes it impossible for me to get to Him.....IF I JUST HANG IN THERE.....HE CAN STILL COME TO ME!!!!!

That sums up my testimony –

- THERE WERE TIMES WHERE I COULDN'T GET TO CHURCH....BUT I AM SO GLAD THE GOD OF THE CHURCH....CAME TO ME......

- THERE HAVE BEEN TIMES WHEN I WAS SHACKLED BY A HEAVY BURDEN....BENEATH THE LOAD OF GUILT & SHAME......THAT I COULDN'T GET TO GOD....BUT I PRAISE GOD....THAT THERE HAS NEVER BEEN A TIME WHERE GOD COULDN'T COME WHERE I WAS!!!!!

The text says...Jesus walks right through that rough wind.... & on that rough water.....and Jesus gets to them....when? @ The 4th watch of the night....

That time is between 3 o'clock & 6 o'clock IN THE MORNING

- It is the time that is most fearful time to many
- It is the time early in the morning when phones don't ring
- It is the time that seems like it would be the worst time of the day

WHAT THE ACCOUNT HERE IS TRYING TO TELL US IS THIS....WHEN IT SEEMS LIKE THE DARKEST MOST DISMAL & DIFFICULT TIME.....the text says......THESE ARE THE TIMES WHEN NO ONE ELSE CAN COME TO OUR RESCUE.....THAT IS WHEN GOD WILL SHOW UP!!!!!

- You may be here....and you are trying to walk towards the Lord.....
- You may be here and you have realized...I need to get to Jesus.....if you are going to walk to Jesus.....
- You need to see the Sovereign is bigger than your situation.

IN FACT: the Bible says....He has been given a name which is above any other name......Philippians 2:9 says...MEANING: WHATEVER NAME YOU CAN NAME.....HIS NAME IS ABOVE IT!!!!!—LET ME PUT IT THIS WAY...WHATEVER PROBLEM YOU CAN NAME....HIS NAME IS ABOVE IT!!!!!

- Whatever the doctors may call it....His name is above it.....I know cancer is big.....but can I tell you that Christ is bigger

Whatever you can name.....His name is above it ALL!!!!

We see the sovereignty of Christ

We see....in order to have DISCOVER GODS AUTHORITY WE MUST ALSO SEE

2. The Strength of Christ---- Vs. 28-29 .....

When they all saw Jesus walking on the water.....Peter says...Lord if it be thou, bid me come unto thee on the water.

& What did Jesus say? COME

PETER IS SAYING....IF I AM GOING TO GET TO YOU LORD....I AM GOING TO NEED YOUR STRENGTH...

If you are going to have AUTHORITY IN CHRIST.....UNDERSTAND THIS.....You & I cannot live a Godly life.....in our own strength!!!!!

- I don't care how strong you think you are....

- I don't care how long you have been in church....you cannot and will not have success walking in your own strength!

God told Zerubabel that he could walk in AUTHORITY....BUT IT WASN'T BY MIGHT –NOT BY POWER---BUT ONLY THROUGH HIS SPIRIT! ------

Peter sees what can be done because Peter sees Jesus walking on the water.....and he WANTS PERMISSION FROM THE SAVIOR SO HE SAYS....Lord, if it is you, bid me come unto thee.....

PETER DOES NOT WANT TO TAKE 1 STEP....UNTIL HE HEARS FROM THE LORD!!!!!

Peter made up his mind....I will not move out of this boat....I don't want to move forward unless you tell me to Lord!!!!!

The biggest mistakes we have ever made....is when we didn't wait on the Lord

SOME OF THE BIGGEST MISTAKES I HAVE EVER MADE...WAS BECAUSE I DIDN'T WAIT ON A WORD FROM THE LORD!!!!

THE BIGGEST MESSES I EVER GOT IN......WAS BECAUSE I DIDN'T WAIT ON GOD

THE TIMES WHEN I CRIED UNNECESSARY TEARS AND WALKED UNNECESSARY FLOORS BECAUSE I DIDN'T WAIT ON A WORD FROM THE LORD

TIMES I PUT MYSELF IN HARMS WAY...... I DON'T WANT TO MOVE UNLESS GOD SPEAKS!!!!

I am not getting out unless you tell me to!!!

WHAT HE IS IMPLYING IS....I won't move until you tell me....BUT OH, IF YOU TELL ME---

- IF you say come--- I will move
- If you say come---I will get out of my comfort zone
- If you say come---I will leave these jokers on the boat
- If you say come--- I will step out!!!!!!

HAVE YOU REACHED THAT POINT IN MATURITY....where IF THE LORD TELLS YOU TO DO SOMETHING...YOU WILL DO IT?:

- If He Tells You To Step---You Will Step
- If He Tells You To Go---You Will Go
- If He Tells You To Stand---You Will Stand

PETER SAID LORD IF IT IS YOU....GIVE ME A WORD!!!! NOW, LOOK WHAT THE WORD WAS!!!!!!

ALL THE LORD SAID WAS......COME!!!!

SIMON PETER MOVED ON THE STRENGTH OF JUST 1 WORD!!!!!

THAT TELLS ME: ......Maturing faith recognizes His voice......and responds without hesitation....

- He jumped out of the boat on 1 word....

- He didn't need a combination of words....he didn't need the Lord to give Him a long speech..... ALL THAT HE NEEDED WAS JUST 1 WORD!!!!!

- How about this he didn't need confirmation of the word.......he didn't discuss it with Andrew or James or anybody else in the boat.....ALL HE NEEDED WAS JUST 1 WORD!!!!

He didn't need the Lord to clarify it or say it again real slow......Peter didn't say...CAN YOU SAY THAT 1 MORE TIME......let me be clear now Lord....you are sure Lord...right.....you are 100% sure.....NO, JESUS SAID COME.....& THE DISCIPLE WENT!!

---MAY I SAY TODAY......WE NEED MORE OF THAT..... WHEN JESUS SAYS IT.....GO ON & DO IT....DONT THINK ABOUT IT...DON'T DISCUSS IT....GET TO DOING WHAT GOD SAID TO DO!!!!!

Do you know what the problem was with the others? THEY DIDN'T EVEN ASK!!!!

SOME BELIEVE IF THEY DON'T ASK....THEN THEY ARE SAFE IN THE BOAT.....BUT LET ME TELL YOU....SOMETHING....THE SECURITY & SAFETY WASN'T IN THE BOAT....IT WAS WITH JESUS!!!!!

All he got was 1 word.....

NOW.....maybe you are setting on the BOW OF THE SHIP....WAITING ON THAT ONE WORD....MAYBE THAT WORD IS HEALED...MAYBE THAT ONE WORD IS....DELIVERED

Settled – Fixed – Approved – Chosen – Done – Forgiven - Loved

THAT IS WHY I DON'T NEED A LIST OF SONGS TO GET ME HAPPY OR A FULL SERMON TO GET ME GOING....JUST 1 WORD FROM THE LORD.....is all I need!!!

WHEN I COME TO CHURCH ---I COME TO PRAISE HIS HOLY NAME.....& LISTEN FOR THAT 1 WORD FROM THE LORD---TO GET ME TO STEP OUT JUST A LITTLE FARTHER!!!---

SIMON PETER SAID....if I am going to walk WITH AUTHORITY....I need your strength ....you see his strength is His Word!!!

So when Jesus says 1 word.....Peter climbs out of the boat & walked on the water.....I WANT TO SUGGEST SOMETHING

It wasn't so much as Peter walking on the water.....AS MUCH AS IT WAS....Peter was walking on the Word....

THE LORD PUT THE WORD OUT TO COME....& WHEN PETER STEPPED OUT OF THAT BOAT...THAT WORD THAT CAME FROM

THE LORD....CARRIED PETER ON TOP OF THAT WATER......SIMON PETER WASN'T WALKING ON THE WATER.....HE WAS WALKING ON THE WORD.....

WHAT I AM SAYING IS......WHENEVER YOU LET GODS HOLY WORD CARRY YOU....YOU WILL NOT FALL...YOU WILL NOT SINK..... WHEN I LET THE WORD OF GOD CARRY ME--------every time I stepped out on faith.....HIS WORD CARRIED ME....WHEN I DECIDED TO COME TO OHIO ....I came on the wings of 1 verse.....TRUST IN THE LORD WITH ALL THINE HEART & LEAN NOT TO THINE OWN UNDERSTANDING....IN ALL THY WAYS ACKNOWLEDGE HIM AND HE SHALL DIRECT THY PATH!!!

- That word has brought me out of so many valleys

- That Word has helped me get through a lot of 4th watches!!!!

WHEN JAMES WAS INSPIRED BY THE HOLY SPIRIT OF GOD TO WRITE THAT BLESSED BOOK.....I have a sneaking suspicion that when he wrote....Be ye doers of the word, and not hearers only.....HE THOUGHT OF PETER WALKING ON THE WATER!!!!.....The Disciple heard THE WORD.....& the Disciple DID THE WORD!!!

AND MY CHALLENGE TO YOU TODAY IS.....DONT JUST HEAR THE WORD.....BE DOERS!!!! PUT IT INTO ACTION.... & STEP OUT OF THE BOAT!!!!!

We see the sovereignty of Christ—NO PROBLEM IS BIGGER THAN GOD---we see the Strength of Christ

WHEN YOU DISCOVER HIS AUTHORITY....

3. We see you can SUMMON CHRIST

Look here in VS.24---- contrary.....against....an antagonistic wind!!!! -----Acting in opposition; opposing, especially mutually------hostile; unfriendly.

I LEARNED AT A VERY YOUNG AGE----- IT ISNT A FRIENDLY WIND....IT IS A CONTRARY WIND......A HOSTILE WIND..... ....A DEMONIC WIND....

IF God allows it...the devil will do it....the boils? The death of Job's family?

The devil did what the devil always does....HE IS GOOD AT DISTRACTING!!!!

WHEN THE DEVIL CAN'T DEFEAT YOU....HE TRIES TO DISTRACT YOU....

Peter is walking on the water.....& HE STOPS SEEING CHRIST.....AND SEES THE CRISIS!!!!

HE WAS DISTRACTED....

HOW DOES THE DEVIL DO THIS? The Devil is nothing like God .....meaning nothing like God in Power....NEVER SAY OUT LOUD WHAT YOU DON'T WANT THE DEVIL TO HEAR.....if that is true...& I believe it is.....THE DEVIL HEARS OUR PRAYERS!!!!!

You pray for a job, and Satan hears this and when you get the job....you get happy but what the devil does is....he manipulates the situation to get you to have a job that takes you out of church!!!!!

I WILL PRAY FOR PEOPLE TO GET A JOB, OR A BETTER ONE.....BUT NOT AT THE EXPENSE OF THEM MISSING CHURCH!!!!

SAME THING WITH A MATE!!!!!

Anything or anybody that distracts you from the Word....is not meant for your life!!!

VS. 30-----Peter saw the wind boisterous!!!!NOT CONTRARY...BUT BOISTEROUS---ROUGH & NOISY ...MIGHTY & STRONG!!!!...THE ONLY TIME THIS IS USED IN SCRIPTURE!!!!!—

THE CLOSER JESUS GOT TO THE DISCIPLES.....THE WORSE THE STORM BECAME!!!!!

GOOD REACTION....HE cried out to God...He shrieked........He called out loud.......HE SUMMONS GOD!!!!

And here in this text...Peter teaches us something.....HE CALLED OUT & PRAYED @ THE BEGINNING OF THE PROBLEM!!!!

AGAIN VS. 30---And beginning to sink

- He Didn't Wait Till The Problem Got Over His Head
- He Didn't Wait Until He Was Going Under For The Last Time....
- He Didn't Wait Until He Was At His Last Breath....

VS. 30 SAYS AT THE BEGINNING....AT THE START.....OF THE PROBLEM....HE CRIED OUT....

WHEN HE NOTICED:

- Things Were Changing...........
- His Status Was Being Altered
- Things Were Not Like They Used To Be

May I suggest.....don't start praying when things are over your head......you must pray FROM the start....

A.   He Didn't Just Pray At The Start Of The Problem.....
B.   He Prayed To The Savior About The Problem

He didn't look back to the boat.... THE ONES IN THE BOAT WERE IN THE SAME SITUATION AND STORM HE WAS!!!!!

So Peter prayed directly to the Lord!!!!!

He opened his mouth and had enough sense to call on somebody who could help him!!!!!

C.   He Prayed About His Problem!!!!

IT IS PETER HIMSELF......THAT KNEW HE NEEDED PRAYER.....AND IT WAS NOT a DRAWN OUT PRAYER----IT WAS A 3 WORD CRY.....THAT SHOOK THE GATES OF HEAVEN!!!!!

DO YOU KNOW WHAT THAT TELLS ME? When it gets dark & difficult.....you will get down to business quick.....

The moment you start talking to God.....THE GOD I SERVE HAS ENOUGH POWER TO ANSWER RIGHT THEN & THERE....& IF YOU ARE LOST....IF YOU ARE SINKING...IF YOU ARE A SINNER WHO HAS NEVER ACCEPTED CHRIST....AND YOU FEEL LIKE YOU ARE GOING UNDER JUST SHOUT......LORD SAVE ME!!!!

My life with Christ can be summed up like this....HE IS A RIGHT ON TIME GOD!!!!!

HE DIDN'T ANSWER WHEN I WANTED HIM....BUT HE CAME RIGHT WHEN I NEEDED HIM!!!!

Look at verse 31---the sweetest 2 words in response to prayer I have ever heard..........And immediately

How many here can be honest and shout glory....that there have been times when you asked God....when you cried out to God...& immediately you knew it was going to be alright?????

You called out.... & God stepped in & turned it around

You cried out to God with all sincerity in your heart……YOU CAN PRAISE GOD RIGHT HERE & NOW….BECAUSE THERE WAS A TIME YOU WERE HUNGRY---HE FED YOU……WHEN YOU WERE THIRSTY ----HE GAVE YOU SOMETHING TO DRINK……..WHEN YOUR BACK WAS AGAINST THE WALL….HE CAME THROUGH

DO YOU KNOW WHAT THAT TELLS ME? THE SAME POWER & AUTHORITY THAT WAS DISPLAYED THAT DAY…..IS THE SAME POWER & AUTHORITY WE CAN EXPERIENCE TODAY!!!!

Now look….When Jesus got in the boat with them….the wind died down….. ….say what you want …think what you want….THIS IS WHAT I GET OUT OF THE TEXT…NOT MADE UP….JUST GOOD OLD COMMON SENSE….when Jesus picked Peter up OUT OF THE WATER….they both had to have walked ON THE WATER …to get IN THE BOAT!!!!—

……EVEN WHEN YOU HAVE FAILED BEFORE….GOD HAS ENOUGH POWER…TO GET YOU BACK UP & BACK ON THE RIGHT TRACK TO THE VERY THING HE TOLD THEM TO DO….GET IN THE BOAT & GO TO THE OTHER SIDE!!!

YOU DON'T HAVE TO LIVE A DEFEATED LIFE……listen…..what must you do to be saved?---Know He is bigger than your problem…..& when you see His Sovereignty ….God has given you a word….to Come….will you? Now, if you feel you are in a difficult place…..---SUMMON HIM….Say Lord, save me!!!!

8

The Letters To The Seven Churches
Revelation 1-3

Robert Prichard
Pastor Cleveland FWB church -- Denominational Officer

As stated earlier in this series, the popular view being presented today is that the Seven Churches represent seven time periods in history from the first Advent of Christ until His return for the Church...that we are now living in the Laodicean age. Because the Scofield Reference Bible has been the favorite study Bible of many since 1910, we are faced with a theory for which there are no Bible facts. Someone said, "...So for twenty years I had taught as a prophecy of God's Word a human conclusion based upon an ambiguous paragraph." He said the only "authority" he had for his belief was a "footnote in my favorite edition of a study Bible." (J. Bray's quote from H. Rimmer)

The breakdown of the time periods of history according to this theory is as follows: Ephesus—30-100 A. D.; Smyrna—100-313 A. D.; Pergamos—313-590 A. D.; Thyatira—590-1517 A. D.; Sardis—1517-1790 A. D.; Philadelphia—1730-1900 A. D.; Laodicea—1900-? (Source: J. Royce Thomason)

Again, note, there is no Scriptural evidence to even hint that these letters describe different time periods. These letters describe conditions which occur in churches over and over...again and again.

I. The Church at Ephesus

(Rev 2:1 KJV) Unto the angel of the church of Ephesus write; These things saith he that holdeth the seven stars in his right hand, who walketh in the midst of the seven golden candlesticks;

(Rev 2:2 KJV) I know thy works, and thy labour, and thy patience, and how thou canst not bear them which are evil: and thou hast tried them which say they are apostles, and are not, and hast found them liars:

(Rev 2:3 KJV) And hast borne, and hast patience, and for my name's sake hast laboured, and hast not fainted.

(Rev 2:4 KJV) Nevertheless I have somewhat against thee, because thou hast left thy first love.

(Rev 2:5 KJV) Remember therefore from whence thou art fallen, and repent, and do the first works; or else I will come unto thee quickly, and will remove thy candlestick out of his place, except thou repent.

(Rev 2:6 KJV) But this thou hast, that thou hatest the deeds of the Nicolaitanes, which I also hate.

(Rev 2:7 KJV) He that hath an ear, let him hear what the Spirit saith unto the churches; To him that overcometh will I give to eat of the tree of life, which is in the midst of the paradise of God.

VERSE 1:

- Remember, the stars are the angels...the angel is God's messenger or spokesman (pastor) to the church.

- "In His right hand" signifies His protection and authority over the pastor.

- "He who walks" says to us that Christ is always active in the affairs of the church...giving grace to the weary and judgment to the rebellious.

VERSE 2:

- "I know thy works"...the good, the bad, the ugly—as they say.

(Psa 139:1 KJV) To the chief Musician, A Psalm of David. O LORD, thou hast searched me, and known me.

(Psa 139:2 KJV) Thou knowest my downsitting and mine uprising, thou understandest my thought afar off.

(Psa 139:3 KJV) Thou compassest my path and my lying down, and art acquainted with all my ways.

(Psa 139:4 KJV) For there is not a word in my tongue, but, lo, O LORD, thou knowest it altogether.

(John 21:17 KJV) He saith unto him the third time, Simon, son of Jonas, lovest thou me? Peter was grieved because he said unto him the third time, Lovest thou me? And he said unto him, Lord, thou knowest all things; thou knowest that I love thee. Jesus saith unto him, Feed my sheep.

- Jesus commends them for their "toil and patience."

- They could spot a hypocrite right away.

- They put them to the test and found them false.

- Every church in every century has been threatened by the infiltration of false teachers.

- As stated earlier, the church in persecution needed to hear Christ say that things are not what they seem... (The same can be said of people; some are not what they seem to be).

VERSE 3:

- They did not quit because of hypocrites—they did not grow weary (faint).

- It's so sad when so many through the years have dropped out of church because they saw somebody do something or say something (something that hurt their feelings).

- These stayed put for His name's sake.

YOU MAY HAVE A THOUSAND REASONS TO QUIT...BUT, ONE REASON IS ENOUGH TO STAY PUT—HIS NAME'S SAKE!!

VERSE 4:

- With all the good Jesus saw, He saw also the not so good.

- He loved them enough to tell them the truth.

- Jesus was saying to them the same thing the Apostle Paul had said in

1 Corinthians 13...in reality, whatever you do in the name of Christ profits nothing if it is not done in love.

- The "first love" Jesus speaks about is that love of total commitment to the Lord...and to each other...they showed when they first accepted Him as Savior.

P. E. Hughes said: "A diminishing of first love, therefore, is an indicator in a decrease in Godliness."

VERSE 5:

- Jesus knew...what they should have known...that all the good works they were doing would soon cease if there is not a return to Godly love.

- A church cannot continue when there is no love...continual fussing and grumbling...lack of trust.

- To "remove the candlestick" is to have Christ give up on a church that refuses to be His light in a city or community.

- The brightest light others will see is that the church members love one another.

(John 13:35 KJV) By this shall all men know that ye are my disciples, if ye have love one to another.

- A church—or individual Christian—who is known for fussing and quarreling dims the light of the Gospel of Christ.

VERSE 6:

- Who the Nicolaitanes were is not really known.

- The Nicolaitane System; the Baalim System (v.14); the Jezebel System (v.20); the Gentile Walk (Eph 4:17); The Babylonian System...all have to do with the helpers of Satan who draw God's people away from Him by the temptation of the flesh and the seduction of the world.

VERSE 7:

- Every person has a responsibility to listen to what he hears from the Lord.

- How can anyone overcome the seduction of the world?

ANSWER: (Rev 12:11 KJV) And they overcame him by the blood of the Lamb, and by the word of their testimony; and they loved not their lives unto the death.

- In the beginning, man's sin cut him off from the Tree of Life...now through the Blood of the Lamb of God man has access to the Tree of Life again.

II. The Church at Smyrna

(Rev 2:8 KJV) And unto the angel of the church in Smyrna write; These things saith the first and the last, which was dead, and is alive;

(Rev 2:9 KJV) I know thy works, and tribulation, and poverty, (but thou art rich) and I know the blasphemy of them which say they are Jews, and are not, but are the synagogue of Satan.

(Rev 2:10 KJV) Fear none of those things which thou shalt suffer: behold, the devil shall cast some of you into prison, that ye may be tried; and ye shall have tribulation ten days: be thou faithful unto death, and I will give thee a crown of life.

(Rev 2:11 KJV) He that hath an ear, let him hear what the Spirit saith unto the churches; He that overcometh shall not be hurt of the second death.

- These were in tribulation and poverty...

- Becoming a Christian meant to sacrifice earthly goods, job, and often life itself.

- Jesus assures them they are "rich".

- The Jews in the flesh are not in the synagogue of God—they are in the synagogue of Satan.

- Although being the physical seed of Abraham, Jews are not the people of God if they reject Jesus.

- Satan's attacks are a testing time for Christians.

- "Ten days" means a short duration of time.

- "Be thou faithful until death" does not only mean until you die...but, even if it costs you your life...be faithful.

III. The Church at Pergamos

(Rev 2:12 KJV) And to the angel of the church in Pergamos write; These things saith he which hath the sharp sword with two edges;

(Rev 2:13 KJV) I know thy works and where thou dwellest, even where Satan's seat is: and thou holdest fast my name, and hast not denied my faith, even in those days wherein Antipas was my faithful martyr, who was slain among you, where Satan dwelleth.

(Rev 2:14 KJV) But I have a few things against thee, because thou hast there them that hold the doctrine of Balaam, who taught Balac to cast a stumblingblock before the children of Israel, to eat things sacrificed unto idols, and to commit fornication.

(Rev 2:15 KJV) So hast thou also them that hold the doctrine of the Nicolaitanes, which thing I hate.

(Rev 2:16 KJV) Repent; or else I will come unto thee quickly, and will fight against them with the sword of my mouth.

(Rev 2:17 KJV) He that hath an ear, let him hear what the Spirit saith unto the churches; To him that overcometh will I give to eat of the hidden manna, and will give him a white stone, and in the stone a new name written, which no man knoweth saving he that receiveth it.

- The Romans had made Pergamos the capitol of the province of Asia.

- As the center of emperor-worship, Christians were asked to offer incense to the image of Caesar saying, "Caesar is Lord."

- Antipas, the faithful witness, was put to death rather than deny his Savior.

- NOTE: The word "witness" and the word "martyr" come from the same Greek word.

- Their big mistake that Jesus had "against" them: They did not exercise discipline against those who took part in ungodly heathen festivals.

- The immorality that believers were exposed to often led them into fornication.

- These idolatrous feasts...where all sorts of lewd and immoral behavior occurred...were totally incompatible with the moral values of the Christian life.

- The church at Pergamos should have warned—and dealt with—their members concerning the dangers of the compromising attitude they had toward these rock concerts...oops! I meant to say idolatrous heathen festivals.

- Note verse 16—repent or else—I, [Jesus] will fight against them with the sword of my mouth (His Word, the Bible).

- Hidden manna is the bread of life that is hidden from those who refuse to repent.

- In the ancient world, a white stone was cast as a vote of acceptance whereas a black stone was a vote of rejection.

- "He that has an ear, let him hear..."—Are you listening?

IV. The Church at Thyatira

(Rev 2:18 KJV) And unto the angel of the church in Thyatira write; These things saith the Son of God, who hath his eyes like unto a flame of fire, and his feet are like fine brass;

(Rev 2:19 KJV) I know thy works, and charity, and service, and faith, and thy patience, and thy works; and the last to be more than the first.

(Rev 2:20 KJV) Notwithstanding I have a few things against thee, because thou sufferest that woman Jezebel, which calleth herself a prophetess, to teach and to seduce my servants to commit fornication, and to eat things sacrificed unto idols.

(Rev 2:21 KJV) And I gave her space to repent of her fornication; and she repented not.

(Rev 2:22 KJV) Behold, I will cast her into a bed, and them that commit adultery with her into great tribulation, except they repent of their deeds.

(Rev 2:23 KJV) And I will kill her children with death; and all the churches shall know that I am he which searcheth the reins and hearts: and I will give unto every one of you according to your works.

(Rev 2:24 KJV) But unto you I say, and unto the rest in Thyatira, as many as have not this doctrine, and which have not known the depths of Satan, as they speak; I will put upon you none other burden.

(Rev 2:25 KJV) But that which ye have already hold fast till I come.

(Rev 2:26 KJV) And he that overcometh, and keepeth my works unto the end, to him will I give power over the nations:

(Rev 2:27 KJV) And he shall rule them with a rod of iron; as the vessels of a potter shall they be broken to shivers: even as I received of my Father.

(Rev 2:28 KJV) And I will give him the morning star.

(Rev 2:29 KJV) He that hath an ear, let him hear what the Spirit saith unto the churches.

- Here, the Son of God identifies Himself...He sees all and will execute absolute judgment with absolute integrity.

- Jesus commends their works, their love, their faith, and their patience—their works seemingly increasing.

- What Jesus had against them: They were allowing "that woman, Jezebel" to influence and seduce them.

- Remember the Jezebel system...worldly seduction.

- "...cast her into a bed" is similar to what we sometimes say—"You've made your own bed, now you have to lay in it."

- Jezebel's "children" are those who allow themselves to be influenced by the fleshly, worldly lifestyle.

- Unless they repent...they face the same fate as Jezebel.

- Note verse 23—"...all the churches shall know..."

- Note verse 24—"...they have not known the depths of Satan..."

Sadly, in America today where it is a crime to recognize God in our schools, our children are only learning the deep things of Satan—such as killing unwanted unborn babies, the sins of Sodom, and the weakening of the sanctity of marriage.

- Because of our union With Christ, we rule with Him...even now.

V. The Church at Sardis

(Rev 3:1 KJV) And unto the angel of the church in Sardis write; These things saith he that hath the seven Spirits of God, and the seven stars; I know thy works, that thou hast a name that thou livest, and art dead.

(Rev 3:2 KJV) Be watchful, and strengthen the things which remain, that are ready to die: for I have not found thy works perfect before God.

(Rev 3:3 KJV) Remember therefore how thou hast received and heard, and hold fast, and repent. If therefore thou shalt not watch, I will come on thee as a thief, and thou shalt not know what hour I will come upon thee.

(Rev 3:4 KJV) Thou hast a few names even in Sardis which have not defiled their garments; and they shall walk with me in white: for they are worthy.

(Rev 3:5 KJV) He that overcometh, the same shall be clothed in white raiment; and I will not blot out his name out of the book of life, but I will confess his name before my Father, and before his angels.

(Rev 3:6 KJV) He that hath an ear, let him hear what the Spirit saith unto the churches.

- There is nothing in this church that Christ can commend.
- They had a name of being a lively church, but...He who knows...said they were dead.
- However, the church as a whole being too referred as dead, had a few faithful ones.
- It is evident here that Christ wants to restore—and will restore—those who are willing to repent.

VI. The Church at Philadelphia

(Rev 3:7 KJV) And to the angel of the church in Philadelphia write; These things saith he that is holy, he that is true, he that hath the key of David, he that openeth, and no man shutteth; and shutteth, and no man openeth;

(Rev 3:8 KJV) I know thy works: behold, I have set before thee an open door, and no man can shut it: for thou hast a little strength, and hast kept my word, and hast not denied my name.

(Rev 3:9 KJV) Behold, I will make them of the synagogue of Satan, which say they are Jews, and are not, but do lie; behold, I will make them to come and worship before thy feet, and to know that I have loved thee.

(Rev 3:10 KJV) Because thou hast kept the word of my patience, I also will keep thee from the hour of temptation, which shall come upon all the world, to try them that dwell upon the earth.

(Rev 3:11 KJV) Behold, I come quickly: hold that fast which thou hast, that no man take thy crown.

(Rev 3:12 KJV) Him that overcometh will I make a pillar in the temple of my God, and he shall go no more out: and I will write upon him the name of my God, and the name of the city of my God, which is new Jerusalem, which cometh down out of heaven from my God: and I will write upon him my new name.

(Rev 3:13 KJV) He that hath an ear, let him hear what the Spirit saith unto the churches.

- "The key of David" speaks of trust and authority.

(Luke 1:32 KJV) He shall be great, and shall be called the Son of the Highest: and the Lord God shall give unto him the throne of his father David:

- "Little strength" indicates this church appeared weak and insignificant.

- However, to this little church God had opened a door of opportunity in the midst of trying circumstances.

- Paul and Barnabas had a door of faith (opportunity) opened:

(Acts 14:27 KJV) And when they were come, and had gathered the church together, they rehearsed all that God had done with them, and how he had opened the door of faith unto the Gentiles.

- God was proving to all the churches…and the world…that He could the use weak to confound the mighty.

(1 Cor 1:27 KJV) But God hath chosen the foolish things of the world to confound the wise; and God hath chosen the weak things of the world to confound the things which are mighty;

- It is not how powerful we are among men…but, how faithful we are before God.

- Compare v. 9 with Isaiah 60:14…

(Isa 60:14 KJV) The sons also of them that afflicted thee shall come bending unto thee; and all they that despised thee shall bow themselves down at the soles of thy feet; and they shall call thee, The city of the LORD, The Zion of the Holy One of Israel.

- This verse seems to be saying that those who have (despised) criticized the ones who do stand for the truth will sooner or later have to confess it—willingly or unwillingly.

- v. 10—these had kept His Word and patiently endured.

- v. 11—"I am coming quickly" means suddenly or at any time.

- v. 12—"I will write on him...the name of my God" is the direct opposite of having the mark of the devil upon one's life.

REMEMBER: WE EITHER HAVE THE MARK OF THE LAMB OR THE MARK OF THE BEAST.

- v. 12—the New Jerusalem is where our citizenship is now.

(Eph 2:20 KJV) And are built upon the foundation of the apostles and prophets, Jesus Christ himself being the chief corner stone;

(Eph 2:21 KJV) In whom all the building fitly framed together groweth unto an holy temple in the Lord:

(1 Pet 2:5 KJV) Ye also, as lively stones, are built up a spiritual house, an holy priesthood, to offer up spiritual sacrifices, acceptable to God by Jesus Christ

(Heb 12:22 KJV) But ye are come unto mount Sion, and unto the city of the living God, the heavenly Jerusalem, and to an innumerable company of angels,

(Heb 12:23 KJV) To the general assembly and church of the firstborn, which are written in heaven, and to God the Judge of all, and to the spirits of just men made perfect,

He that hath an ear, let him hear what the Spirit saith unto the churches.

VII. The Church at Laodicea

(Rev 3:14 KJV) And unto the angel of the church of the Laodiceans write; These things saith the Amen, the faithful and true witness, the beginning of the creation of God;

(Rev 3:15 KJV) I know thy works, that thou art neither cold nor hot: I would thou wert cold or hot.

(Rev 3:16 KJV) So then because thou art lukewarm, and neither cold nor hot, I will spue thee out of my mouth.

(Rev 3:17 KJV) Because thou sayest, I am rich, and increased with goods, and have need of nothing; and knowest not that thou art wretched, and miserable, and poor, and blind, and naked:

(Rev 3:18 KJV) I counsel thee to buy of me gold tried in the fire, that thou mayest be rich; and white raiment, that thou mayest be clothed, and that the shame of thy nakedness do not appear; and anoint thine eyes with eyesalve, that thou mayest see.

(Rev 3:19 KJV) As many as I love, I rebuke and chasten: be zealous therefore, and repent.

(Rev 3:20 KJV) Behold, I stand at the door, and knock: if any man hear my voice, and open the door, I will come in to him, and will sup with him, and he with me.

(Rev 3:21 KJV) To him that overcometh will I grant to sit with me in my throne, even as I also overcame, and am set down with my Father in his throne.

(Rev 3:22 KJV) He that hath an ear, let him hear what the Spirit saith unto the churches.

- v. 14—"Amen" signifies what is firm and true.

- v. 14—"the beginning of the creation of God" designates Jesus as the Creator.

- v. 15—"I know thy works"…nothing escapes Him.

- v. 15—The "lukewarm" person is the hardest person to work with.

- Lukewarm people bore easily.

- Because of the "lukewarmness" of the Laodicean people, they were not worthy of the Lord Jesus—whose Name they claimed.

- They knew nothing of cross-bearing.

- v. 16—NOTE: The Lord can…and does…become grieved or angry with people—but, that does not seem to be the indication here.

- When He says "I will spue" them out of His mouth…He is not speaking as one who is grieved or angry, but one who is thoroughly disgusted.

- To "spue" out literally means to vomit…as sick to the stomach.

- Jesus was disgusted with those whose religion was a mere pretense or show.

(Amos 6:1 KJV) Woe to them that are at ease in Zion, and trust in the mountain of Samaria, which are named chief of the nations, to whom the house of Israel came!

- v. 17—They were rich and prosperous…having become very proud hearted…conceited…and defiant.

- Theirs was not so much a "holier than thou attitude" as it was a "better than thou attitude".

- They were so conceited they could not see that they were poor, wretched, miserable, naked, and blind.
- They were dressed in the finest clothing...but, shamefully unclothed in the presence of God...Their righteousness was as "filthy rags".
  - v. 18—"gold refined by fire" represents true wealth.
  - "white garments" is symbolic of Christ's righteousness.

(Isa 64:6 KJV) But we are all as an unclean thing, and all our righteousnesses are as filthy rags; and we all do fade as a leaf; and our iniquities, like the wind, have taken us away.

- It is said that making and selling eye salve was a prosperous business...hence, Jesus said they needed their eyes anointed with His eyesalve that they might see.
- v. 19—What a comforting thought...those with whom Jesus is thoroughly disgusted...He says, "...as many as I love, I rebuke and chasten".
- He says be "zealous" and repent. Note: zealous means to "boil" or "inflame"

(Rev 3:20 KJV) Behold, I stand at the door, and knock: if any man hear my voice, and open the door, I will come in to him, and will sup with him, and he with me.

9
Things That Hinder Our Prayers

Tom Dooley
Pastor Austintown FWB church -- Clerk State Association

A few years ago, a severe storm that produced 70-80 mile an hour winds ripped its way over our house in Glenn Heights, TX. During that intense storm, I called my brother to warn him and his family that a possible tornado was headed their way.

However, when he answered the phone, the line became static and then it went dead. That was a very scary time because I lost all communication to warn my loved ones of a possible tornado.

1.   But let me tell you something that is 100 times worse than not being able to communicate with your family when the phone lines are down--not being able to get through to God in prayer.

2.   When we pray to God, we want Him to hear our prayers without any static in the prayer line. We want to have our prayers heard without anything interfering with them.

I WANT TO SHARE WITH YOU THREE THINGS THAT CAN HINDER OUR PRAYERS TO GOD.

I. First, An Unforgiving Spirit Can Hinder Our Prayers To God.

(Mk. 11:25) "And when you stand praying, if you hold anything against anyone, forgive him, so that your Father in heaven may forgive you your sins."

1. Jesus is telling us that God will not forgive us of our sins unless we forgive others when they sin against us. So in other words, our prayer for forgiveness can be denied if we are holding grudges against others. An unforgiving spirit can hinder our prayers to God.

ILLUSTRATION:

John Oglethorpe, in talking to John Wesley, once made the comment, "I never forgive." Mr. Wesley wisely replied, "Then, sir, I hope that you never sin."

2. If we want our sins forgiven and our prayers to reach God without any hindrances, we must have a forgiving spirit! We must forgive even when someone doesn't deserve it.

(Eph. 4:31-32) "Get rid of all bitterness, rage, and anger, brawling, and slander, along with every form of malice. Be kind and compassionate to one another, forgiving each other, just as in Christ God forgave you."

ILLUSTRATION:

A good example of someone who forgave others when they did not deserve it is the story of Joseph and his brothers.

Joseph, who was the eleventh of Jacob's twelve sons, and the firstborn son of Rachel, was grossly mistreated by some of the members of his family. First of all, his own brothers wanted to kill him because of a dream he had that pointed out that someday his whole family would bow down to the ground before him. However, instead of killing him, a few of his brothers sold Joseph as a slave to a caravan of Ishmaelite's who were on their way to Egypt. While in Egypt, we read that Joseph spent years in prison because of false accusations of Potiphar's wife who said that Joseph made improper advances toward her.

All in all, Joseph's experienced many hardships. He was betrayed by his family, kidnapped, enslaved, and imprisoned. This is a man who had every right to have bitterness and anger toward his brothers.

However, we read in (Gen. 45:14-15) that when Joseph was reunited with his brothers in Egypt, "he threw his arms around his brother Benjamin and wept, and Benjamin embraced him, weeping. And he kissed all his brothers and wept over them."

Although his brothers had been unfaithful to him, he graciously forgave them and shared his prosperity with them.

3. If Joseph somehow found the strength to forgive others when they mistreated him, we too can find the strength to forgive those who have mistreated us. We must forgive so that our prayers will not be hindered toward God.

II. Second, An Improper Husband-Wife Relationship Can Hinder Our Prayers To God.

(1 Peter 3:7) "Husbands, in the same way be considerate as you live with your wives, and treat them with respect as the weaker partner and as heirs with you of the gracious gift of life, so that nothing will hinder your prayers."

1. This verse teaches that if a man is not considerate and respectful towards his wife, his prayers will be hindered. If a husband does not treat his wife with love, honor, and respect,

which she deserves, it is my option that he does not deserve to have his prayers considered by God.

2. An improper husband-wife relationship hinders prayer because to have a good relationship with God depends on right relationships with others. If we do not have a right relationship with others, then our relationship with God is affected.

ILLUSTRATION:

A while back, I saw a story on TV about a Minister who worked at a productive church and was supposedly a successful man of God. During the program, he confessed that for years he would come home from a hard day's work and take out his frustrations on his wife. He just didn't verbally abuse her, but he physically beat her and on several occasions he almost killed her.

3. If you were God, would you want to hear and answer this man's prayer? Absolutely Not.

4. If we mistreat our spouse, God may not consider our prayers.

III.   Lastly, Doubt Can Hinder Our Prayers To God.

(Jam 1:5-7) "If any of you lacks wisdom, he should ask God, who gives generously to all without finding fault, and it will be given to him. But when he asks, he must believe and not doubt, because he who doubts is like a wave of the sea, blown and tossed by the wind. That man should not think he will receive anything from the Lord; he is a double-minded man, unstable in all he does."

1.	Doubt means, "to be undecided or skeptical about something." It is a lack of certainty and lack of trust! As Christians, doubt is an enemy to our faith because we are to believe what God has said will happen. If we doubt God's ability to answer our prayers, then He won't answer them.

ILLUSTRATION:

In (Luke 1), we are introduced to two people--Zechariah who was a priest during the time of Herod king of Judea, and his wife Elizabeth. They were both very godly people who served the Lord. However, there was one thing that was lacking in their lives. They wanted a child. However, Elizabeth was barren and they were both well along in years. Over a course of time, they prayed earnestly for a child and God heard their prayers and sent an angel to them to announce the good news that He was going to grant them a child.

However, in (Luke 1:18f), Zechariah doubted and did not believe the news that the angel brought from God. Because Zechariah doubted God's promise, he was taught a lesson. He was not able to speak until the day the child was born.

2.	When we ask God for something, but deep down in our hearts we doubt that we will receive it, He teaches us a lesson by not granting our prayer requests. Doubt hinders our prayers.

3.	Let us strive to have the kind of faith that Jesus commissions us to have in (Mk. 11:22-24).

"Have faith in God," Jesus answered. "I tell you the truth, if anyone says to this mountain, 'Go, throw yourselves in the sea,' and does not doubt in his heart but believes that what he says will happen, it will be done for him. Therefore I tell you, whatever you ask for in prayer, believe that you have received it, and it will be yours."

4.	When we pray, let us pray with mountain moving faith. We must believe that we will receive what we ask for. Doubt kills prayer, faith on the other hand brings prayer to life.

CONCLUSION:

1.	Prayer is one of the great blessings we have as Christians. We need to be living such a good life that ensures that our prayers are going directly to the throne room of God without any interferences.

2.	Here are three things that can hinder our prayers to God:

a.	An unforgiving spirit.
b.	An improper husband-wife relationship.
c.	Doubt.

3.	If you struggle with these things, then get them repaired today, so that your prayer lines of communication will be smooth and static free.

10

When Is A Preacher A Failure
II Timothy 4:1-8

Tim Stout
Pastor Heritage FWB church -- Home Mission Board

God has a plan to accomplish His will. His plan is "preaching." *He calls* men to this task and those He calls are to respond by doing as *He commands*!

1. **The Charge From The Master.**

We are charged to be proper stewards of His Word and His Gospel. Paul's charge to his son in the ministry is infamous with this thought!

2 Timothy 4:1-5 (KJV) *¹ I charge thee therefore before God, and the Lord Jesus Christ, who shall judge the quick and the dead at his appearing and his kingdom; ² <u>Preach the word</u>; be instant in season, out of season; reprove, rebuke, exhort with all longsuffering and doctrine. ³ For the time will come when they will not endure sound doctrine; but after their own lusts shall they heap to themselves teachers, having itching ears; ⁴ And they shall turn away their ears from the truth, and shall be turned unto fables. ⁵ But watch thou in all things, endure afflictions, do the work of an evangelist, <u>make full proof of thy ministry</u>.*

The Master has called us to ministry, not merchandising. We are not called to *tickle* the ear, but to *tell* the message!

In this passage, we are taught to be faithful to...
- **The Master** - we need to work every day on our relationship with our Master!
- **The Message** - His message will not change and we need to be faithful to Him, His Word and His text; preaching His Word in its context!
- **The Motive** - we love Him and serve Him because he first loved us and gave Himself for us!
- **The Ministry** - what he has called us to do!

Several years ago I read a poem that has inspired to a great truth about ministry. I believe it is titled, **A Job Or A Ministry.**

Some people have a job in the church;
Others involve themselves in a ministry.
What's the difference?
If you are doing it because no one else will, it's a job.
If you are doing it to serve the Lord, it's a ministry.
If you quit because somebody criticized you,
It was a job.
If you keep on serving, it's a ministry.
If you'll do it only as long as it does not interfere
With your other activities, it's a job.
If you are committed to staying with
It even when it means
Letting go other things; it's a ministry.
If you quit because no one praised you or thanked you;
it was a job.

If you stay with it even though nobody recognizes your efforts;
it's a ministry.
It's hard to get excited about a job.
It's almost impossible not
To be excited about a ministry.
If our concern is success, it's a job.
If our concern is faithfulness, it's a ministry.
An average church is filled with people doing jobs.
A great and growing church is
Filled with people involved in ministry.

Where do we fit in? What about us?

If God calls you to a ministry, don't treat it like a job.
If you have a job, give it up and find a ministry.
God does not want us feeling stuck with a job,
But excited and faithful to Him in a ministry.

I want to lift two phrases from our text and speak concerning them today.

> **_Preach the word_.** The Word is the infallible, inerrant, indestructible and inspired Word. It does not need re-written but re-read! Preach <u>His</u> Word. Declare <u>His</u> truths, not your opinion or philosophies. God did not call us to entertain but to preach His truth! To convince people of His truth and you reprove them with His Word! Rebuke them as needed ~ tell them what is right and what is wrong. Let your preaching be led of God's Holy Spirit and always filled with love and compassion!

Paul was thankful for God's call to salvation; to serve and to share the Gospel (I Timothy 1:11-12). Paul in turn committed this same

Gospel to Timothy (I Timothy 6:20); and Timothy was charged to present it to faithful men who would also teach and preach the Word (II Timothy 2:2).

> ### **_Make full proof of thy ministry._**
> As you labor for Him, you will minister to others. God called you and that will have to sustain you when people get tired of hearing you!
>
> Barnes says of this passage… The word here used denotes, properly, to bear or bring fully; then to persuade fully; and then to make fully assured of, to give full proof of. The meaning here seems to be, *to furnish full evidence of what is the design of the Christian ministry, and of what it is adapted to accomplish*, by the faithful performance of all its duties.
>
> Timothy was so to discharge the duties of his office as to furnish a fair illustration of what the ministry could do, and thus to show the wisdom of the Savior in its institution. This should be the aim of all the ministers of the gospel. Each one should resolve, by the blessing of God that the ministry, in his hands, shall be allowed, *by a fair trial*, to show to the utmost what it is adapted to do for the welfare of mankind.
>
> This is the charge from the Master - preach His Word and make full proof of thy ministry!
>
> I want to insert a personal note right here. Please pray for your pastor! The pastorate is a difficult place to be,

no matter how much you love your people and no matter how much they love you, real ministry is tough!

Today we fight against the "wiles of the devil" inside the church instead of "woes of evil" outside of the church.

The modern church wants
- Heaven without Hell.
- Music without Majesty. They want to appeal to the flesh and not the heart!
- A Loving Jesus without a Judging Lord.
- They want to hear about Christ but not a commitment to Church. That's church membership without church workmanship!
- They want to have faith and believe but they don't want to repent and convert from being a sinful life.

That's why Paul said to Timothy 1 Timothy 6:12 *"Fight the good fight of faith, lay hold on eternal life,"* And Jude said it this way... Jude 1:3-4 *Beloved, when I gave all diligence to write unto you of the common salvation, it was needful for me to write unto you, and exhort you that ye should <u>earnestly contend for the faith</u> which was once delivered unto the saints.* [4] *For there are certain men crept in unawares, who were before of old ordained to this condemnation, ungodly men, turning the grace of our God into <u>lasciviousness</u>, and denying the only Lord God, and our Lord Jesus Christ.*

2. **The Character Of The Minister.**

There is no question about the *charge* presented by Apostle Paul.

However, many question the *character* of the minister. The word character is a word that speaks to the set of qualities that make somebody or something distinctive. It also speaks to what you really are.

I use it in this point to speak how one acts or even reacts to others. There will be some things that happen in the ministry that cause others to label you as successful of unsuccessful.

Let me explain, *some may suggest you are a failure when...*
 A. **People leave the church you pastor.** However, people come and go. Many followed Christ for the miracles but when the food was gone, so were they (John 6:66).
 B. **People are not getting saved.** I wish people got saved every service; I wish I led folks to Christ each week and had someone walking the aisle confessing Christ; I wish the baptistery was used each week – but that doesn't always happen! Thank God when it does! Ask Noah or Jeremiah about this – the key is staying faithful and God will bless. You sow the seed – it is God that gives the increase (I Corinthians 3:7). I am not justifying barren altars but I am saying it is God who does the saving and I should not be discouraged...but encouraged to be faithful in His cause!
 C. **Problems and pressures are great**. When the burdens are heavy and you can't eat or sleep; the schedule is hectic and you seem to be spinning your wheels – keep going for Jesus!
 D. **Pay is inadequate.** Others have things and you lack - others eat out and you can't afford to go. Remember, some people don't care and some churches can do no more (Matthew 6:33). Your goal is to please God no matter how meager the pay!

Don't let these things get you down – you are not a failure because your car is old and has no hub caps; your suit don't fit well or you have to put cardboard in your shoes to keep your feet from falling out the bottom of them. Many men have had great success in ministry while their appearance left something to be desired!

You have heart and character and feed the flock of God! Live in *His strength* and stay in *His Scriptures*!

But YOU WILL BE A FAILURE IF….

A. <u>**You compromise to please the hearers instead of pleasing God.**</u> Live a life of love and compassion and preach with love, but never compromise the Scriptures! If you preach against sin – they will say "amen." When you name sin – they will accuse you of meddling; preach it anyway! Remember to patiently reprove and rebuke in love.
B. <u>**Your preaching is "wishy-washy.**</u> Ephesians 4 reminds us *That we henceforth be no more children, tossed to and fro, and carried about with every wind of doctrine, by the sleight of men, and cunning craftiness, whereby they lie in wait to deceive;*
C. <u>**Your preaching is void of love and compassion**</u>. 1 Corinthians 13:1 (NKJV) *Though I speak with the tongues of men and of angels, but have not love, I have become sounding brass or a clanging cymbal.* Don't preach without love or while you are mad! People need God and God is love. You will not win them if you don't love them!
D. <u>**Your heart is not burdened for souls.**</u> Romans 10:1 (KJV) *Brethren, my heart's desire and prayer to God for Israel is, that they might be saved.* The Lord is still inviting souls

to be saved (Revelation 22:17) and God still desires souls to be saved (II Peter 3:9). People don't care how much you know till they know how much you care!

E. **Fail to point people to Christ**. This is His ministry and it's all about Him! Romans 10:8-14 (NKJV) *⁸ But what does it say? "The word is near you, in your mouth and in your heart" (that is, the word of faith which we preach): ⁹ that if you confess with your mouth the Lord Jesus and believe in your heart that God has raised Him from the dead, you will be saved. ¹⁰ For with the heart one believes unto righteousness, and with the mouth confession is made unto salvation. ¹¹ For the Scripture says, "Whoever believes on Him will not be put to shame." ¹² For there is no distinction between Jew and Greek, for the same Lord over all is rich to all who call upon Him. ¹³ For "whoever calls on the name of the Lord shall be saved." ¹⁴ How then shall they call on Him in whom they have not believed? <u>And how shall they believe in Him of whom they have not heard? And how shall they hear without a preacher?</u>*

YOU WILL BE A FAILURE IF....

F. **Preach messages to please listeners instead of being led by Holy Spirit**. We must not rely on the "wisdom of man" but must on the "power of the Spirit." Preaching is not to be polished without power but fervent and fundamental.

G. **Ethics are dishonest**. As you pray and prepare to preach, be honest in your heart and preach what "thus saith the Lord." Make an effort to get along with all and don't bad mouth people (even if it's true☺).

H. **Unfaithful to your wife and children**. 1 Timothy 3:2 (NKJV) *A bishop then must be blameless, the husband of one wife,...*Daily nurture your relationship to Christ, your companion and your children. Be careful in counseling and how you handle yourself with others.

YOU WILL BE A FAILURE IF....

I. **Your children disrespect you.** God allowed me to raise 3 wonderful children that respect me – I gave them no reason not to! Live your faith in front of them; don't speak negative about the ministry or people you minister to. 1 Timothy 3:4 (NKJV) *one who rules his own house well, having his children in submission with all reverence*

J. **Pay is more important than obedience.** Not every church can take care of a pastor the way they should! But you go, you stay where God places you and never let "pay and packages" enter into the picture. 1 Timothy 6:10 (NKJV) *For the love of money is a root of all kinds of evil, for which some have strayed from the faith in their greediness, and pierced themselves through with many sorrows.*

God has placed me where I am – I will never doubt that! I want God to use me for His glory. I am His servant; a saved soldier of the cross of Christ.

John Newton said, "You have desired a good work--may the Lord give you the desires of your heart. May He give you...

- the *wisdom* of Daniel,
- the *meekness* of Moses,
- the *courage* of Joshua,
- the *zeal* of Paul,
- And that *self-abasement* and *humility* which Job and Isaiah felt--when they not only had *heard* of Him by the hearing of the ear--but when they *saw* His glory, and abhorred themselves in dust and ashes!

May you be taught of God for none teaches like Him and come forth an able minister of the New Covenant, well instructed rightly to divide and faithfully to distribute the Word of truth.

In the *school of Christ*, you will have to learn some lessons which are not very pleasant to flesh and blood. You must learn to *labor*, to *run*, to *fight*, to *wrestle* and many other hard exercises; some of which will try your strength, and others your patience.

Another said...You know the common expression, *'a jack of all trades'*. I am sure a minister had needed be such a one:
- a brave *soldier,*
- an alert *watchman,*
- a caring *shepherd,*
- a hardworking *farmer,*
- a skillful *builder,*
- a wise *counselor,*
- a competent *physician,*
- And a loving *nurse.*

Do not be discouraged - you have a wonderful and a gracious *Master*, who does not only give *instructions*--but *power* and *ability!* He engages that His grace shall be sufficient, at all *times* and in all *circumstances*, for those who simply give themselves up to His teaching and His service.

"Be an example to all believers . . ." 1 Timothy 4:12
- in what you teach,
- in the way you *live,*
- In your *love,* your *faith,* and your *purity."*

There is much involved in being a shepherd. Several times I have been asked by children the question, "Pastor, what do you do besides preach at our Church?" I always offer the obvious answers...
- I visit the sick people and home, nursing facilities and hospitals.
- I help people go through tough times in their lives when they have problems at home; at their work or even at school.
- I am there when someone in the family passes away.
- I think you too get the picture. I minister to others!

I know you really don't want to "hear what I believe" but I must say I wonder if the reason so many pastors are quitting; not staying the course; not finishing the task is because we "feel" we have so much to get done that we fail to really accomplish what God has called us to do!

I want to finish this message with some startling statistics I recently learned:
- The Barna Research Group reports *1,500 clergy leaving pastoral ministry each month.*
- Christianity Today said *61% of congregations have forced a pastor to leave.*
- Hartford Institute for Religious Research says *83% of clergy spouses want their spouse to leave pastoral ministry.*
- U.S. Bureau of Labor and Statistics says *90% of clergy in all denominations will not stay in ministry long enough to reach the age of retirement.*
- Hartford Institute for Religious Research says *50% of pastors indicated that they would leave the ministry if they had another way of making a living.*

I am greatly concerned that we spend much time in multi-tasking and not effectively accomplishing anything!

D. L. Moody said, "This one thing I do...., not these 40 things I dabble in."

If God has called us to shepherd, then what's a shepherd to do?

Several years ago a poll was taken among preachers concerning the different duties of the ministry. The top 6 answers were as follows.
1) Administration.
2) Teaching.
3) Preaching.
4) Pastoring.
5) Priestly Work.
6) Church Business

Then 2 follow-up questions were asked;

First Question: "What do you think is the most important of these ministries?" An overwhelming response was "Preaching."
Second question: "Which occupies most of your time?" Again, an overwhelming answer: "Administration."

I believe I can see from this what has happened. We know the importance of preparation, intervention, visitation and administration, yet I am afraid more time is spent doing those things than intercession, supplication, and presentation and preaching of the Lord's Gospel!

The Word of God is powerful and convicts souls, converts lives, challenges us for daily living yet we spend more time on programs instead of preaching; we try entertainment instead of exhorting and edifying with the Word; we try counseling instead of asking the Holy Spirit to bring caution, comfort and conviction from the Word of God!

May God help us to be faithful to preach His Gospel! Paul said, _Preach the word;_ and _make full proof of thy ministry_.

Here's the application. I am a human doing a spiritual work. It is not easy and few seem to truly understand.

However, this is God's Work and He will be the One to get credit and glory....I am just to be a faithful servant in _Preaching the word;_ and _making full proof of thy ministry_.

11
Hold On
Hebrews 4:14-16

Louis Nettleton
Pastor Williams Road FWB church

Hebrews 4:14-16, 14: Also, let's hold on to the confession since we have a great high priest who passed through the heavens, who is Jesus, God's Son; 15 because we don't have a high priest who can't sympathize with our weaknesses but instead one who was tempted in every way that we are, except without sin. 16 Finally, let's draw near to the throne of favor with confidence so that we can receive mercy and find grace when we need help.

Introduction

Hebrews 2:17 Therefore, he had to be made like his brothers and sisters in every way. This was so that he could become a merciful and faithful high priest in things relating to God, in order to wipe away the sins of the people.

Jesus Christ put on flesh becoming like us in every way so we could not point our finger towards God and declaring His inability to understand mankind's struggle. Jesus putting on flesh not for His sake but for us knowing He had faced the struggles of the flesh, knowing He could be just towards mankind, knowing He was a righteous and understanding High Priest.

Outline;

Vs. 14 ...also, let's hold on to the confession since we have a great high priest who passed through the heavens, who is Jesus, God's Son;

A.   Jesus is the High Priest of our Confession in the shed blood of Jesus, His death, and Resurrection giving victory over the greatest of all our fears... Death.

Romans 3: 9 because if you confess with your mouth "Jesus is Lord" and in your heart you have faith that God raised him from the dead, you will be saved. 10 Trusting with the heart leads to righteousness, and confessing with the mouth leads to salvation. 11 The scripture says, all who have faith in him won't be put to shame. 12 There is no distinction between Jew and Greek, because the same Lord is Lord of all, who gives richly to all who call on him. 13 All who call on the Lord's name will be saved. (Hold on to the confession of our faith. Anchor the mind to the truth of God's word.)

Romans 7: 21 So I find that, as a rule, when I want to do what is good, evil is right there with me. 22 I gladly agree with the Law on the inside, 23 but I see a different law at work in my body. It wages a war against the law of my mind and takes me prisoner with the law of sin that is in my body. 24 I'm a miserable human being. Who will deliver me from this dead corpse? 25 Thank God through Jesus Christ our Lord! So then I'm a slave to God's Law in my mind, but I'm a slave to sin's law in my body. *(The front line of the battle is not in the flesh but the mind our minds must be filled with the knowledge of God. The light of God word drives out the darkness. As heavenly knowledge increases darkness decreases.)*

Galatians 6:9 Let's not get tired of doing good, because in time we'll have a harvest if we don't give up. (The strength of our grip is rooted not just in the knowledge of God's word but in loving service living to touch hearts trapped in the darkness of this World.)

Colossians 3:1 Therefore, if you were raised with Christ, look for the things that are above where Christ is sitting at God's right side. 2 Think about the things above and not things on earth. 3 You died, and your life is hidden with Christ in God. 4 When Christ, who is your life, is revealed, then you also will be revealed with him in glory. 5 So put to death the parts of your life that belong to the earth, such as sexual immorality, moral corruption, lust, evil desire, and greed (which is idolatry). (The work of Jesus Christ is finished, power has been provided for your journey, and victory awaits those who persevere unto the end. [Matthew 24:12-14])

I. Worthy High Priest

Hebrews 1:3-4, (Jesus is all powerful, the essence of Righteousness, and greater than the angels

Hebrews 1:13, (He is the mighty right hand of God and is more powerful than any of our enemies)

Hebrews 2:9, (Stepped down from Heaven put on flesh, faced death but triumphed over death and the grave [I Corinthians 15:57] and now crowned with Glory.)

Hebrews 3:1, (The Apostle and High Priest of our confession, greater than Moses and builder of everything)

Hebrews 2:11-18, (Not ashamed of us, I will publicly announce your name to my brothers and sisters. I will praise you in the middle of the assembly. He has set us free from the fear of death, and has wiped away the sins of His people.)

Vs. 15 ...because we don't have a high priest who can't sympathize with our weaknesses but instead one who was tempted in every way that we are, except without sin.

A. **He understands our weakness**

1. II Corinthians 12:9 He said to me, "My grace is enough for you, because power is made perfect in weakness." So I'll gladly spend my time bragging about my weaknesses so that Christ's power can rest on me. (Grace carries us through our weakness allowing us to grow stronger. The real question is, "Do we trust in the power of God?")
2. Psalm 34:17 When the righteous cry out, the LORD listens; he delivers them from all their troubles. 18 The LORD is close to the brokenhearted; he saves those whose spirits are crushed. 19 The righteous have many problems, but the LORD delivers them from every one. (He can deliver, bind up the brokenhearted, delivers you from the jaws of the prey, nothing defeats our God.)
3. I Corinthians 10:13 No temptation has seized you that isn't common for people. But God is faithful. He won't allow you to be tempted beyond your abilities. Instead, with the temptation, God will also supply a way out so that you will be able to endure it. (Perseverance is key to your deliverance. God enable us to persevere!)
4. Hebrews 2:1 & 4:1 ([...Lest you drift away & Hold on] God will be faithful to do His part we must be faithful to our part to stay close to God to ensure victory).

B. **Tempted but without sin!**

Vs. 16 Finally, let's draw near to the throne of favor with confidence so that we can receive mercy and find grace when we need help.

A. **Draw near to God's throne**

   1. James 4:8 Come near to God, and he will come near to you. Wash your hands, you sinners. Purify your hearts, you double-minded. (The closer we draw to God the brighter the light of God is in us. With each portion of spiritual knowledge the darkness within grows weaker. The knowledge of God adds more power to our diligent pursuit of God.)
   2. Hebrews 7:25 This is why he can completely save those who are approaching God through him... (He is the great High Priest able to deliver us unto the Father as we pursue Him!)
   3. Revelation 15:4 Who won't fear you, Lord, and glorify your name? You alone are holy. All nations will come and fall down in worship before you, for your acts of justice have been revealed." (His power is complete!!)

B. **The throne of Grace, Mercy, Favor...**

   1. James 4:6-7 But he gives us more grace. This is why it says, God stands against the proud, but favors the humble. 7 Therefore, submit to God. Resist the devil, and he will run away from you. (There is no shortage of Grace but remember that grace is made stronger in our lives as we submit to God and resist the Devil.)
   2. Psalm 5:12 because you, LORD, bless the righteous. You cover them with favor like a shield. (The favor of rest upon the righteous it becomes our covering our comfort/peace and joy.)
   3. Proverbs 3:1-4 My son, don't forget my instruction. Let your heart guard my commands,

2 because they will help you live a long time and provide you with well-being. 3 Don't let loyalty and faithfulness leave you. Bind them on your neck; write them on the tablet of your heart. 4 Then you will find favor and approval in the eyes of God and humanity. (Hold fast the commands of God, faithfulness to God's Word bring great favor in the midst of our journey)

C.   Grace in the time of our need...

1. Romans 6:12-14 so then don't let sin rule your body, so that you do what it wants. 13 Don't offer parts of your body to sin, to be used as weapons to do wrong. Instead, present yourselves to God as people who have been brought back to life from the dead, and offer all the parts of your body to God to be used as weapons to do right. 14 Sin will have no power over you, because you aren't under Law but under grace. (Not only grace to cover us when we fall but grace to be weapons or tools in the hands of God bringing light to a dark and hopeless World.)
2. II Corinthians 8:6-7 As a result, we challenged Titus to finish this work of grace with you the way he had started it. 7 Be the best in this work of grace in the same way that you are the best in everything, such as faith, speech, knowledge, total commitment, and the love we inspired in you. (The work of Grace is not ended in us but is meant to flow through us into others about us. The greatest work of Grace is about loving, especially those undeserving.)

Conclusion; In order to see the full work of our High Priest we must look at the eight "I AM," statements found in the book of John;

    Water of Life, John 4:14
    Bread of Life, John 6:35 & 58
    I AM the Good Shepherd, John 10:11 & 14
    Light of the World, John 8:12
    The Way, Truth, and Life, John 14:6
    The Door, John 10:9
    The Resurrection, John 11:25
    I AM the Vine, John 15:5

12

THE POOR WISE MAN
And
OTHER FORGOTTEN HEROES
Ecclesiastes 9:11-18

Mike Mounts
Pastor Harrison FWB church -- State Board of Directors

INTRODUCTION

He wore #7 on the back of his pin-striped jersey. At that time the NY Yankees were on TV nearly every Saturday. I can still remember when as a boy I used to sit in front of that old large cabinet, black and white TV, and watch Bobby Richardson, Elston Howard, Clete Boyer, Roger Maris (#9), and Mickey Mantle (#7). What a duo: Mantle and Maris. I'll never forget Dad taking me to a spring training game in Bradenton, Florida, where I actually had the privilege of seeing Mantle play. In 1956 he won the Triple Crown when he batted .353, hit 52 home runs, and had 130 RBIs. He won 3 MVPs and 4 home run titles. He was inducted into the Baseball Hall of Fame in 1974.

I could just picture myself, one day playing for the Yankees and getting to wear a pin-striped uniform before thousands of people in historic Yankee Stadium. I could just hear baseball commentators, Dizzy Dean and Pee Wee Reese call out my name. Mantle was my hero. I wanted to be just like him.

He wore #14. His nickname was "Charlie Hustle." He could play about any position and what an exciting player to watch. He had speed. He played outfield and infield. He developed the head-first slide. Even when he got a base-on-balls, he still ran to first base. He was a switch hitter, and boy what a hitter! On Sept. 11, 1985, at Riverfront Stadium, Pete Rose got his 4,192 hit, to break Ty Cobb's record. Pete ended his career with 4,256 hits. I had the privilege of seeing him play at old Crosley Field, as well as at Riverfront Stadium. Pete was my hero.

Webster defines a hero "as anyone admired for their courage, nobility, or exploits. Anyone admired for their qualities or achievements and *regarded as an ideal or model.*"

Mantle had tremendous athletic ability and is a baseball legend, and what achievements! But I only saw what he was on the field. I didn't know that off the field he had a serious drinking problem and was an alcoholic. There were games in which he actually played drunk or with a hangover. He was hardly the ideal role model. I certainly didn't need to pattern my life after him.

Then there's good old "Charlie Hustle." He was a "hustler" all right. Because he liked to gamble and bet on sports events (even baseball), Pete Rose will never be inducted into Cooperstown. He, too, was hardly the ideal role model.

Notice how Solomon describes what are and are not admirable qualities of a hero.

> Note: Eccl. 9:11. Heroism is not based on:
> Who's the fastest?
> Who's the strongest?

Who's the cleverest?
Who's the richest?
Who's the most popular?

Truth is, the athlete super-star, the most ingenious, the wealthiest, and the most popular person in the world are subject to circumstances which lie beyond their control: "Time and chance happen to them all" (v. 11f). For the athlete it could be an injury or charges of domestic violence, as with Ray Rice. A stock market crash could be devastating to people like Bill Gates, Warren Buffet, or the Koch brothers. This year's America Idol winner better enjoy it while he can; there will be another one take his place next year. Popularity comes and goes.

In spite of a person's present status, life, or career (they may even appear to be invincible) their time on earth can suddenly and unexpectedly expire, "like fish taken in a cruel net, [and] like birds caught in a snare" (v. 12). Then of course, there is the divine and providential hand of God, who ultimately is in control. Truth is, no matter how hard he may try, man is never fully "master of his own fate and captain of his own soul." There are far too many factors and variables.

Heroism isn't even based on:

Who's the prettiest?
Who's the most handsome?
Who's the best known, or who has the most to say.

Note: Eccl. 9:13-18. True heroism is based:

- On godly wisdom and character (that's the emphasis in the text).
- On what a person is on the inside.
- A true hero is willing to remain anonymous (v. 15a).
- A true hero doesn't need to be recognized (v. 15a).

- A true hero doesn't need to be remembered (v. 15b)
- A true hero doesn't need to be rewarded.

Just as the old saying goes, "You can't judge a book by its cover," neither can you judge a person simply by their outward appearance. Notice the contrasts in our text:

A great king	A poor wise man
Wealthy	Poor
Garments of royalty	Garments of poverty
Impressive	Common
Commanding presence	Unassuming
Gave commands	Gave wisdom
Weapons of war	Weapon of wisdom

Here is this little town with a few men, being bullied and surrounded by this great and wealthy king, along with his well-trained army. But the great king had finally met his match: a poor wise man!

At age 39, he was struck down with polio. His arms, back, and hands became partially paralyzed. Despite a worsening physical condition and the urging of many to retire from his political career, he fought back and wouldn't give up. During the depths of the Great Depression and at the age of 51, Franklin Delano Roosevelt became president of the United States. He was actually re-elected three more terms. He served as president during WWII and died shortly before its end. No matter what you think of his politics or policies, he was a man who just wouldn't give up.

He was almost totally deaf from childhood. But at the age of 30, Thomas Edison invented the phonograph. His other inventions were the light bulb, microphone, and movies.

He was born in poverty, and his formal schooling totaled less than a year. But he gave himself an education, and through hard work he became a respected lawyer. Although he was tall and lanky, uncomfortable before an audience, spoke in a slow high-pitched voice, and was defeated six times for political office, Abraham Lincoln became 16th President of the United States.

He was a short, hunch-backed man, with poor eyesight. He wasn't an eloquent speaker, nor did he have a commanding presence. His enemies regularly questioned his motives and ministry and called him a deceiver and false prophet. He was so hated that chains and tribulation awaited him in every city. Although he spent quite a bit of time in jail, the apostle Paul became the greatest missionary the world has ever known.

In spite of the pitfalls, inconsistencies, and immoral behavior of so many athletic figures, Hollywood stars, and music artists, in most cases, these individuals have more impact on the thinking, values, and culture of our young people than a year of Sunday School does. That's why as parents it's up to you to make sure your kids know more about Dr. Luke than they do Dr. Phil.

The Book of James (a book on Christian ethics) needs to be more popular with our children than Lebron James. Our daughters and granddaughters need to learn more about great women like Queen Esther, Ruth, Abigail, Lydia, Priscilla, and missionaries like Elizabeth Elliott, Amy Carmichael, and Free Will Baptist's own Laura Bell Barnard.

Solomon was right. True heroes are often forgotten, unappreciated, unrewarded, despised, and even ignored. Do you think the poor wise man said to himself, "I'll be a hero and one day they'll read about me in the Bible"? Did the five marines who raised the US flag over Iwo Jima in February 1945, do so in order to forever be memorialized in history? A true hero doesn't set out to be a hero. They simply do the heroic, whether they get the credit or not. That's true heroism.

The poor wise man of Ecclesiastes 9, though not praised of men, was praised of God. Though not rewarded by men, was rewarded by God. Although he was forgotten by men, he was remembered by God. And although poor in this world, he was rich in faith.

As a believer, who are your role models? Who are your heroes? Are you basing your choices by the world's venue or a Christian worldview? What sort of role model are you? Is it merely outward show, or is it godly wisdom and internal character? After all, God is always most interested in the heart.

While preparing today's sermon, I got to thinking about certain people God has brought into my life. These people have had a major impact on my life, and although not with us today, still have an impact. There is my First Grade teacher, Frances Carter. I learned much more from her than just reading, writing, and arithmetic.

My Fifth Grade teacher and principal, Naomi Miller, made learning fun and exciting. She was a woman of velvet steel.

Carl Brown taught me a lot of great guitar "licks." Boy! Could he ever play the guitar!

Robert Meade, my pastor after Sandy and I married, showed me what passion for Christ and His Word looks like not only in the pulpit but also in practice.

David Martyn Lloyd-Jones, although I have never met him and is at home today with the Lord, still stirs my soul as I read his sermons. It's as if every page is on fire!

There's an old country boy by the name of Harrison Sullivan that I came to know and greatly respect while pastoring in Alabama. What a godly man! A humble man. The fact that I was a "Yankee" from Ohio didn't bother him a bit. In fact, that sort of thing never came up in our conversations. I sat and listened closely as he told me story after story of when he served under General Patton during WWII. It was amazing as he recalled specific dates, places and events. As I think back, although he was several years my elder, had experienced such historical events, and was a highly decorated soldier, he respected me too. I learned more from him than just history.

He was born on May 24, 1917, in a little cabin house in the hills of eastern Kentucky. He was one of seven children. Because of hard times and the size of the family, he went to work and only received a fourth-grade education. He served during WWII from 1943-1946 as a Crew Chief in the US Air Force. Shortly after returning home, he was saved. In the early fifties he was called to preach and ordained to the ministry. He started two churches and salvaged at least two others that were about to close their doors. His last pastorate was the church where he was saved years earlier.

Need I say more? My dad is among my greatest heroes. I never took the opportunity to tell him so before he died. That's one of the problems when it comes to real heroes; we take them for granted. We seem to never truly appreciate them until they're gone. Dad never saw himself as a hero, but that's the way heroes are. You can be right in their presence and not even know it. Well, when it comes to my father, I know it now. And perhaps one day when I get to heaven, I'll get another opportunity to tell him.

And to those of you with us today who bravely served our nation: "Thank you!" Our hats off to you. Thank you for protecting the freedom and liberty we enjoy today as Americans. Personally, I wish to thank you. Although I've never been in the military myself, I greatly admire and respect any man or woman who has bravely served our country. And every chance I get, when I see a veteran, I thank them no matter when or where they served. I am grateful for the opportunity to proclaim the Word of God to you today without any outside resistance or threat on our lives. What a blessed privilege! But it has not come without a price.

Conclusion

Several years ago I was asked to preach in chapel service at Genoa Christian Academy, where Sandy used to teach. I asked the pre-school through fifth grade students, "What is a hero?" One little girl answered, "A hero is someone who saves the world." What an answer, especially when it comes to the greatest Hero who ever lived.

He lived in poverty, "on the other side of the tracks," and was reared in obscurity. He possessed neither wealth nor influence. He didn't have an imposing outward appearance. He didn't look like a hero. His relatives were inconspicuous, and He had neither training nor formal education. He did "not cry out, nor raise His voice, nor cause His voice to be heard in the street" (Isa. 42:2). He didn't try to stir up a following or force His way into power. Even those within His own family resented and rejected Him. Many ignored His words, valued His worth at the price of a common slave, despised and rejected Him, and rewarded Him with crucifixion. Yet He committed the results to His Father.

Today, many have forgotten Him and others have used His name as a byword or swear word. But just like any hero, He didn't come to make a name for Himself. He came to glorify the name of His Father.

"Therefore God also has highly exalted Him and given Him the name which is above every name, that at the name of Jesus every knee should bow, of those in heaven, and of those on earth, and of those under the earth, and that every tongue should confess that Jesus Christ is Lord, to the glory of God the Father" (Phil 2:9-11).

He's the ultimate Hero! He's my hero. He's the One I wish to pattern my life after and to follow in His steps (1 Pet. 2:21b). What qualities! What accomplishments! What a Savior!

13

How To Spoil Everyone's Day and Ruin Your Life
Numbers 11

Aaron Reid
Pastor Sciotodale FWB church

INTRODUCTION
If someone asked you, "What is the most common sin in the world?" What would you say?

- Anger?
- Lust?
- Hatred?
- Envy?
- Covetousness?

No doubt those sins make the "Top Ten" list of common sins, but there is one sin that outranks most, if not all other sins. It is the sin of complaining.

Yes, I said, complaining.

Complaining is so commonplace that most of us probably don't think of it as a sin, if we think about it at all.

I read the other day that recently Facebook actually considered changing its name to Gripe book, but Facebook founder, Mark Zuckerberg decided against it. Personally, I think it could be a good idea considering the number of posts that seem to be nothing more than gripe sessions about this or that.

But most of us don't really think that we complain very much, when the reality is that it's just easier to see it in others. If we complain, it's just showing genuine concern. If someone else complains, it's a gripe session.

So, do you complain?

Have you complained about anything today?

- Did you gripe about the weather?

- Did you complain about the drive to work or to church – maybe someone ahead of you driving too slowly, or because he didn't use his turning signal?

- Did you complain because someone said something mean to you, or because you couldn't find the right outfit, or because someone else got to the shower before you and used all the hot water?

Would you still say that you haven't complained today?

One final question – *If I asked your family or friends or whoever you've been with so far this morning would they also say that you absolutely complained about nothing today?*

Probably not, because it's likely we've complained about something. After all, most of time, when we do complain, we don't even realize that that's what we're doing. And we do it without considering the danger we put ourselves in by doing it.

Yet, complaining is dangerous; for it is a sin that can have potentially devastating consequences.

To understand, open your Bible to 1Corinthians 10:1-12... "Moreover, brethren, I would not that ye should be ignorant, how that all our fathers were under the cloud, and all passed through the sea; And were all baptized unto Moses in the cloud and in the sea; And did all eat the same spiritual meat; And did all drink the same spiritual drink: for they drank of that spiritual Rock that followed them: and that Rock was Christ.

But with many of them God was not well pleased: for they were overthrown in the wilderness.

Now these things were our examples, to the intent we should not lust after evil things, as they also lusted. Neither be ye idolaters, as were some of them; as it is written, the people sat down to eat and drink, and rose up to play. Neither let us commit fornication, as some of them committed, and fell in one day three and twenty thousand. Neither let us tempt Christ, as some of them also tempted, and were destroyed of serpents.

Neither murmur ye, as some of them also murmured, and were destroyed of the destroyer.

Now all these things happened unto them for ensamples: and they are written for our admonition, upon whom the ends of the world are come. Wherefore let him that thinketh he standeth take heed lest he fall

When God set Israel free from Egyptian slavery, he carried them away on 'eagle's wings'. He led them out by a pillar of cloud by day and fire by night. He took them through the Red Sea, which

He parted with a mighty wind, and as He led them through the wilderness, he gave them food to eat and water to drink.

He met their every need, physical and spiritual, as the text implies.

And yet, as they journeyed along they fell out of favor with God for the many sins they committed; sins that Paul names in verses 6-10:

They lusted after evil things...
They worshipped idols...
They committed fornication...
They tempted Christ...

And, finally, they murmured. Notice verse 10 again…. "Neither murmur ye, as some of them also murmured, and were destroyed of the destroyer."

Paul names five sins, and for each sin, its consequence, a few of which carried severe consequences. For example, 23,000 died in one day for committing fornication and worshipping idols with the Moabite people. On another occasion, many died from serpent bites for tempting Christ. And finally, many were destroyed for a sin Paul calls "murmuring".

Ya'll know what that is, right? The word simply means, "To grumble".

Scholars are hard pressed to nail down the exact occasion of this sin and resultant judgment, because it happened on more than one occasion. But one such occasion we find in the book of Numbers, chapter 11. And that's where I want to look this morning.

Setting: They children of Israel had been camped out at Sinai for nearly a year, and now they were on the move again. They had the Law and the Ark of the Covenant, and they were moving when God said, "move" and resting when He said "rest". Now, they'd gone three days journey into the desert when they took their first stop, and we find ourselves in chapter 11.

And here we learn several powerful life lessons about the sin of complaining; the first of which is:

COMPLAINING DISPLEASES THE LORD (VS. 1-3)
"And when the people complained, it displeased the LORD: and the LORD heard it; and his anger was kindled; and the fire of the LORD burnt among them, and consumed them that were in the uttermost parts of the camp. And the people cried unto Moses; and when Moses prayed unto the LORD, the fire was quenched. And he called the name of the place Taberah: because the fire of the LORD burnt among them."

If you notice, the text doesn't even tell us what they were complaining about. But do we even need a reason? If someone is given to complaining all the time, you'd be hard-pressed to find a valid reason for every complaint they utter.

And Israel was like that; they complained all the time. In fact, you can trace their complaining, like ant trail, from spot to spot, all the way back to the very first instance when they griped at Moses after he'd went in to talk to Pharaoh the first time.

These people were given to complaining all the time, about anything and everything.

Adam Clarke writes that St. Jerome believed that their chief complaint this time was the *length of the journey*. "It's too hard *to get up and walk so far every day, then unpack the tent, set it up, wait while, and do it all over again the next day!"*

But something Israel may not have remembered is that <u>God always hears what we say</u>. (vs 1)

Even if they whispered it beneath their breath or spoke of it alone in their tents between just husband and wife, God could hear their griping. "The LORD heard it..." and it displeased Him and made Him angry.

Why was God angry? Because complaining was a personal sin against Him.

It was God who brought them out of Egypt and carried them along, and to complain was to raise their voice against Him.

Complaining is a sin, and like any other sin, it merits judgment. You know, that's something we would do well to remember: we cannot sin with impunity. We cannot sin and think that we've gotten by with something, just because we haven't seen the consequence yet.

"The wages of sin is death" and sin always comes with a hefty price tag. When Adam and Eve sinned, the LORD pronounced death, but if you recall, they lived to be over 900 years old, and had to endure hardship, suffering, and violence, and many other forms of difficulty over their lifetime; and all because of sin.

Truth is we cannot begin to calculate the cost of our sin until we look at Mt. Calvary, where Jesus suffered and died. Only there can sin's true cost be seen.

And all sin comes with a high price tag, whether it's murder, rape, robbery, or – even complaining; and complaining displeases and angers God because it is an offense against His sovereignty and providence.

I'll say more about that later, but notice also that...

COMPLAINING LEADS TO OTHER SINS (VS. 4-6)
"And the mixed multitude that was among them fell a lusting: and the children of Israel also wept again, and said, Who shall give us flesh to eat? We remember the fish, which we did eat in Egypt freely; the cucumbers, and the melons, and the leeks, and the onions, and the garlic: but now our soul is dried away: there is nothing at all, beside this manna, before our eyes.

Now, you have to understand that what we're reading in verse 4-6 is a completely different event than what happened in verses 1-3. Understand the enormity of that! They no more finish one sin and suffer the consequences then they're right back doing the same thing again!

Do they ever learn? But we're just like them sometimes, right? We complain about something and maybe we realize we're doing it, so we stop, but a short while later, we're doing it again. It's like a constant battle to keep from griping, right?

Complaining is an insidious sin; it creeps and sneaks up on us, and we're doing it before we know it. But that's not the worst part – the worst part is that complaining often leads to other, even more damaging sins.

In Israel's case, complaining led to the sister-sins of discontent and lust (covetousness). Notice that it says that the "mixed multitude that was among them fell a lusting..." Their complaining led to discontent. *"Who will give us flesh to eat?"* They say is, *"We remember the fish we got for free in Egypt..."* Yeah, well apparently they'd forgotten about the whips, the chains, and the back-breaking labor from dawn to dusk every day.

Apparently they'd forgotten the cruelty of their taskmasters, who denied them straw and required more and more every day and pulled their children from play and forced them to work, who robbed them of their later years, killing them young under the burden of the brick.

God had given them freedom, and they would trade it for the promise of a mouthful of tasty food. The truth is that they weren't any better than Esau, who for a morsel of bread and bowl of stew, sold his birthright, despising the inheritance of God.

They said *"Our souls pine away..."* as if God was allowing them starve to death, when He was providing food for them free of charge, every single day!

Now notice Exodus 16:1-5...

"And they took their journey from Elim, and all the congregation of the children of Israel came into the wilderness of Sin, which is between Elim and Sinai, on the fifteenth day of the second month after their departing out of the land of Egypt.

And the whole congregation of the children of Israel murmured against Moses and Aaron in the wilderness: And the children of Israel said unto them, Would to God we had died by the hand of the LORD in the land of Egypt, when we sat by the flesh pots, and when we did eat bread to the full; for ye have brought us forth into this wilderness, to kill this whole assembly with hunger.

Then said the LORD unto Moses, Behold, I will rain bread from heaven for you; and the people shall go out and gather a certain rate every day, that I may prove them, whether they will walk in my law, or no.

And it shall come to pass, that on the sixth day they shall prepare that which they bring in; and it shall be twice as much as they gather daily."

God gave Israel "manna", a miraculous grain-like substance, from heaven every single day. All they had to do was go out, gather it up, and prepare it into cakes and eat it. No one knew what it was. It looked like coriander seed and had a honey/olive oil flavor. And it was nourishing and life-sustaining.

Verses 7-9
"And the manna was as coriander seed, and the color thereof as the color of bdellium. And the people went about, and gathered it, and ground it in mills, or beat it in a mortar, and baked it in pans, and made cakes of it: and the taste of it was as the taste of fresh oil. And when the dew fell upon the camp in the night, the manna fell upon it."

Their complaining in Numbers 11 was not rooted in reality. They were not starving nor were they malnourished. They simply missed the variety of flavors and textures that Egyptian food provided.

I can understand that. But to complain against God and accuse Him of mistreating them by allowing them to be malnourished (which was a lie) was the height of sin!

This often happens when we begin to complain. Rarely does complaining lay alone in the bed of sin. It often leads to other sins like lust, discontent, anger, bitterness, theft, and a host of other things.

We must guard our hearts against a complaining spirit because ingratitude is among the greatest of sins.

But that's not all. There is a third lesson to learn here...

COMPLAINING IS CONTAGIOUS

Do you know that yawning is contagious? Scientists and behaviorists have learned that every vertebrate yawns, including snakes and lizards! They don't understand why we yawn (although they have several theories) and they don't understand why among some species, such as humans, chimpanzees, and possibly dogs, yawning appears to be *contagious.*

In studying our yawning, scientists have theorized that yawning is a shared experience promoting social bonding. They've also discovered that the level of contagion depends on the intimacy of the relationship. Those closest to us are more likely to "catch" our yawns.

Yes, yawning is contagious; but it seems from our text that complaining is as well!

In verse 4 we read, "And the mixed multitude that was among them fell a lusting: and the children of Israel also wept again…"

The "mixed multitude", as it's called in verse 4, are first mentioned in Exodus 12:38 as people of various ethnic groups that traveled with Israel out of Egypt. Perhaps they were also persecuted people, slaves, or maybe they were Jewish converts, or servants of the Israelites.

Regardless, there were many of them and they were the initial source of complaining on this occasion. They "fell a lusting" after the delicacies of Egypt. But soon, the people of Israel were lusting and complaining with them.

But it didn't stop there. No, because griping is like a bad case of the flu; it spreads everywhere, infecting everyone!

We see who else caught the 'bug' in verses 10-15... "Then Moses heard the people weep throughout their families, every man in the door of his tent: and the anger of the LORD was kindled greatly; Moses also was displeased. And Moses said unto the LORD, Wherefore hast thou afflicted thy servant? And wherefore have I not found favor in thy sight, that thou layest the burden of all this people upon me?

Have I conceived all this people? Have I begotten them, that thou shouldest say unto me, Carry them in thy bosom, as a nursing father beareth the sucking child, unto the land which thou swarest unto their fathers?

Whence should I have flesh to give unto all this people? For they weep unto me, saying, Give us flesh, that we may eat. I am not able to bear all this people alone, because it is too heavy for me. And if thou deal thus with me, kill me, I pray thee, out of hand, if I have found favor in thy sight; and let me not see my wretchedness.

Moses heard the crying and saw the people at their tent doors griping about the lack of fresh fish and other food, and it says, *"Moses was displeased"*. These two words hardly convey the level of angst in Moses' heart at that moment.

The word "displeased" is translated from a word in Hebrew that means, *"...to spoil, by breaking to pieces..."* Moses was angry and frustrated, and soon he began to complain.

Such is the destructive power of complaining! It spoils you and spreads to others, spoiling them too.

Have you ever been around someone who does nothing but complain? What do you want to do? You want to get away from them as quickly as possible, because if you don't, pretty soon your attitude is ruined too.

Moses was worn down by their complaining and his spirit was broken within him.

There is a lesson here for all of us:

For children: Don't complain when you don't get what you want. Your parents work hard to care for you. They do things for you and make sacrifices for you that you probably won't appreciate until you are grown. Please, be thankful so you won't wear them down and break their spirits.

For the employee: Don't gripe on the job – it spoils morale among your co-workers and can negatively affect production. It may even cost you your job.

For the church member: Please don't grumble when things aren't as you would like – it brings a bitter spirit in the church, spoiling the love and peace God wants us to have.

COMPLAINING IS A TERRIBLE SIN

Complaining is the direct consequence of ingratitude, which is really a 'casual despising' of God's sovereignty and providence.

It's like saying, *"God is running things, but He's not doing that good of a job and I think I could do it better."* It's like saying, *"What God has done for me and given to me isn't good enough."*

Would you even dare say those things to God? Of course not! Yet, that is the sentiment in our hearts when we are ungrateful to God and to others.

We gripe and complain because we truly feel, deep down (though we'd never admit it) that what God has done for us is not good enough.

Is it any wonder God reacted so strongly to the sin of complaining?

And He does react!

COMPLAINING INVITES JUDGMENT
Verses 1-3 are a startling example of what can happen when God is angry because of sin. We read that "His anger was kindled; and the fire of the LORD burnt among them, and consumed them that were in the uttermost parts of the camp."

Perhaps we feel He is too harsh. Perhaps we feel the punishment does not fit the crime. That is because we do not understand the *sinfulness* of sin. Sin (all sin) is heinous and worthy of God's wrath. All sin invites His displeasure and judgment.

Complaining is something we do regularly, so we have become desensitized to its evil. But God is holy, and every sin to Him is an offence of the highest order, worthy of death. (Romans 6:23)

Does God still judge sin as He did then? We don't see it plainly, do we? Fire isn't falling; people are not dying, so we go right on complaining.

But remember this: justice delayed is still justice served.

So what are we to do in light of what we observe from this tragic moment in Israel's history?

We are to learn: "Now all these things happened unto them for ensamples: and they are written for our admonition, upon whom the ends of the world are come. Wherefore let him that thinketh he standeth take heed lest he fall." (1Corinthians 10:11-12)

CONCLUSION

As we celebrate Thanksgiving and Christmas, let us practice being thankful for all things in all circumstances. Let's make a real effort at curbing complaining so we don't spoil other people's day, and ruin our own lives.

Paul wrote, "In everything give thanks, for this is the will of God in Christ Jesus concerning you" (1Thessalonians 5:18). You will be a more joyful Christian if you learn the secret of being free from complaining!

14

The Unsinkable Ship
Matthew 8:23-27

Freddy W. Dutton, Th.D. – Full-Time Evangelist

INTRODUCTION:
Open your Bibles to the Book of Matthew, Chapter 8:23-27

Verse 23: And when He was entered into a ship, His disciples followed Him.
Verse 24: And behold, there arose a great tempest in the sea, in so much that the ship was covered with the waves, but He was asleep.
Verse 25: And his disciples came to him and awoke him, saying, "Lord, save us we perish."
Verse 26: And He saith unto them, "Why are ye so fearful, O yea, of little faith". Then he arose and rebuked the wind and sea and there was a great calm.

The Lord and His disciples boarded a boat. Jesus fell asleep and suddenly a storm arose quickly and swept with fury over the Sea of Galilee. The waves arose and were lashed by the violence of the wind. The ship was covered with the waves, so that it was now full of water. When a ship is full of water, it goes to the bottom. But not that ship!

No waters can swallow the ship where lies the Master of oceans and earths and skies.

Every ship in history can sink but not "THIS SHIP", which carried the Creator of all things. The disciples marveled and said, "What manner of man is this that even the winds and sea obey Him". (Matt. 8:27)

A sense of peace swept over their souls, when the Captain assuaged their fears.

Many years ago as a little boy growing up in Virginia, my mother Told me of a great ship called, "The Titanic" My mother's Aunt was missing, and she told me the story about how they thought she could have been on the ship, The Titanic.

There were many large and famous ships in the early 1900's. One was the Britanica, which was a sister ship to the Titanic. She was launched in 1915 and sank in November of 1916 with great loss of life. Another great ship was the mighty Bismarck, the greatest battleship of all time. This German battleship was sunk on her maiden voyage in 1940. An old World War I Era plane with cloth covered wings dropped a torpedo and damaged the steering system which led to the demise of this great ship.

The greatest and most famous of all of the ships was the **H. M. S. TITANIC**. She was the fastest and largest ship of all times. The overall length of this ship was 882.5 feet long. She was 11 stories tall from the water line to the very top.
This ship was built with a double bottom 5 to 6 feet deep. There were 15 water tight compartments. So, if one failed, there would be 14 more.

The anchor of this great ship weighed 15.5 tons. This ship was magnificent to say the least. There was a great chandelier in the grand room with a beautiful wood spiral staircase. This ship was a picture of luxury. No expense was held back. On board were some of the most wealthy people of that day.

There was John Jacob Aster who was worth 150 million dollars. There were famous men on board, like Archibald Bell, aide to President Taft. Also on board was Benjamin Gunheunim, who was worth 95 million dollars. Another wealthy man was Isadore Straus worth 56 million dollars. The owner of the White Star Line was also on board, Bruce Ismaye. He was worth 40 million dollars. There were hundreds and hundreds of immigrants in the second and third class of the ship setting sail for a new world and a new life in America.

I. Man Boasted That This Ship Was Unsinkable And Even God, Himself, Could Not Sink This Ship

Man seemed to be saying, "God, we don't need you anymore"! We're masters of our own destiny. They had bowed down to the shrine of their own ingenuity. They seemed to be saying, "We have finally arrived, and we don't need God anymore".
How tragic when people fail to recognize God, and can dare think they can make it without him.

On that cold night, on April 12, 1912, at 11:40 p.m. traveling at 18 knots, the Titanic struck an iceberg off the coast of Newfoundland and sank to the bottom in two hours and 40 minutes taking 1,640 souls into eternity.

A. FACT DEFEATS THEORY
THEORY SAID, with all the calculations, the Titanic would not Sink.

But **THE FACT IS,** it did sink in two hours and 40 minutes and went to the bottom.

THEORY SAID, there were no icebergs in the area.

But **THE FACT** is, that they were already sailing through large icebergs.

THEORY SAID, the double wall could not be compromised

But, **THE FACT** is, that the side of ship split open like a can when it hit the iceberg.

THEORY SAID, the lookouts would be able to give ample warning.

But **THE FACT** is, that warning was given and was not heeded.

THEORY SAID, 66,000 tons traveling at 18 knots would cut through anything.

THE FACT is, that the ship hit the iceberg with 947,000 ft. tons and split the side of the ship open.

THEORY SAYS, no one will know my sins

THE FACT is, "BE SURE YOUR SINS WILL FIND YOU OUT"!

THEORY SAYS, "I CAN MAKE IT ON MY OWN. I DON'T NEED GOD".

FACT IS, "Not By Works Of Righteousness We Have Done, But According To His Mercy He Has Saved Us."

THEORY SAYS, A God of love would never send me to hell.

But **THE FACT IS,** "That In Hell He Lifted Up His Eyes Being In Torment."

THEORY SAYS, IF WE GO TO HELL, WE WILL HAVE A PARTY.

But **THE FACT IS,** "THAT HELL IS A PLACE OF WEEPING, WHALING, AND GHASHING OF TEETH."

B. THE FOLLY OF UNBELIEF
Why are men lost? Is it because they drink a little liquor, or indulge in cursing or lusting. NO! NO! NO! It is because they fail to believe that God sent His only begotten Son into the world that whosoever believeth on Him might be saved.

Jesus rebuked the disciples and said unto them. "Oh ye of little faith. And why is it that you have not faith. The problem they faced in 1912 is the same problem we face in 2015,"UNBELIEF".

C. THE FOLLY OF UNCONCERN
There were three warnings sent from the crow's nest of The Titanic to the officers on the bridge. However, they took no heed and seemed to be unconcerned. There were six warnings sent from the Marconi Wireless from other ships indicating there were icebergs in the area. The wireless operator responded and said, Shut up, I'm busy"! THIS SOUNDS LIKE TODAY!

D. THE FOLLY OF UNPREPAREDNESS
There were only 20 lifeboats on board the great ship, The Titanic. If they were full, only 1,100 people could be saved. This meant that there were 1,200 doomed from the very beginning. THEY WERE TOTALLY UNPREPARED!

1. The lifeboats had no officers assigned to them.
2. There was no water on board.
3. There were no compasses to give directions.
4. The plugs in the bottoms of the lifeboats had been removed from some of the boats.

II. OTHER SHIPS CLOSE BY
History states that within a 150 mile radius there were ten other ships that could have responded to the Titanic's distress signal on this tragic night.

A. The nearest ship to the Titanic was the "SAMSON" which was anchored only eight miles away. But, she did not respond.

A Congressional hearing was held 40 years later and determined that the "SAMSON" saw the flares. However, they did not respond and sailed away.

Captain Kendrick Nace was asked at the Congressional Hearing, did you see the flares that were sent up by the Titanic. He answered, "Yes". He was also asked, did you understand what these flares meant? He answered, "Yes, the universal call of distress". The Congressional Record reads and I quote, "MY GOD IN HEAVEN, WHY DIDN'T YOU TELL SOMEBODY"? His answer, "Because we were carrying illegal cargo on board. This is very interesting because Samson's life in the Bible, was also wrecked by illegal cargo. His lifestyle was immoral and he was living loosely with the opposite sex.

Illegal Cargo can also be wealth and just busy living this life. WHICH SHIP ARE YOU ON?

B. THE NEXT SHIP WAS THE CALIFORNIAN
The Californian was anchored 18 miles away.
There were many people standing out on deck and saw the flares and realized there was a tragedy taking place.

One man, Ernest Gill, appeared before Congress and was asked the question, What were you doing that night? He said, "I came up on deck and lit up a cigarette. I looked on the horizon and saw the burst of the flares". They asked Mr. Gill, did you understand what that meant and what did you do? He answered, "I flipped my cigarette into the ocean and went back to the boiler room and figured it wasn't any of my business".

That night, many other people went to a comfortable bed while 1,600 plus people were drowning in the icy ocean of the Atlantic just a few miles away.

IT IS MY BUSINESS IF MEN DIE AND GO TO HELL!

At 18 miles away, the Californian could have traveled 18 to 20 knots and could have saved them all, but went to bed.

C. THE NEXT SHIP WAS THE CARPATHEY
The Carpathey was anchored 28 miles away and was shut down for the night.
The Captain of the Carpathey was Captain Ralston. He had already retired for the night and was already in his quarters asleep. The officer in charge was Officer Bissert. He saw the flares and immediately ran down to Captain Ralston's quarters barging in without knocking. He cried out, "Ship in distress, ship in distress"! Captain Ralston immediately took control and began giving orders.
"Full Speed Ahead! Wake Up The Cooks, Get The Doctors Ready, And Prepare To Take On Survivors"!

The Carpathey set sail full speed toward the Titanic. First Officer, James Bissert, was at the wheel sailing through those icy waters. The Congressmen asked him, "Sir, did you realize you were sailing into dangerous waters"? He answered and said, "My hands were sweating, and my heart was racing, but I kept her at full speed". The Congressional Record states: "How did you manage to keep your courage"? Mr. Bissert answered, "I looked over to my right and I saw Captain Ralston with his head bowed, his eyes were closed and his lips were moving"

"I KNEW HE WAS TALKING TO THE CAPTAIN OF THE SEA".
"Wherefore, sirs, I took courage and we sailed on."

Rescue The Perishing,
Care For The Dying
Snatch Them In Pity
From Sin And The Grave
Weep O'er The Eering Ones
Lift Up The Fallen
Tell Them Of Jesus
The Might To Save.

That night the Carpathey rescued all the remaining survivors of those remaining in the water.

May God help us to take courage and reach out to the lost that they may board "THE OLD SHIP OF ZION"!

Won't You Trust Christ This Very Day And Receive
Jesus Into Your Heart!

Amen And Amen

15
Why I Am A Free Will Baptist

Edwin Hayes
Executive-Secretary of the
Ohio State Association of Free Will Baptists

Several years ago when I was pastoring at Columbus First FWB, I heard a sermon on "Why I Am a Free Will Baptist" by Brother Roy Thomas, former director for FWB National Home Missions. It really spoke to me. Later I developed a sermon on the subject and then a lesson I have been teaching across the state. The following article is a compilation of this lesson.

I think there are times in our lives when we should evaluate what we are doing and our motive for doing it. This is true of our church and our denomination. Have you ever thought about why you are a Free Will Baptist? Tradition? Friendships? Location of the church? First of all, I am a Christian, a follower of Jesus Christ. Nothing supersedes this! A denomination should be a vehicle to serve the Lord in a greater way. Our goal is not to build a denomination, but the kingdom of the Lord.

In this day that we live in, it is popular to be "non-denominational" but to be honest I do not know what "non-denominational" means or stands for! I do know, however what Free Will Baptist's stand for! The main reason I am a FWB is what we stand for, our beliefs, our doctrine.

Many today are choosing a church that has the best programs, the most dynamic music or the most exciting worship. However, the greatest reason we should have for attending a church is, what is the message of that church? What is being preached and taught at that church? Nothing is more important than that!

There are many who would say that what the sign says over our doors doesn't matter, but, I for one, believe that signs and labels are important. Labels sure are important when we go to the grocery store!

There are many good Bible believing churches that preach the Gospel who are not Free Will Baptist. Any Bible believing church will have basic beliefs: 1) Inspiration of Scripture. 2) The Virgin Birth. 3) The Deity of Jesus Christ. 4) The Second Coming of Jesus Christ. 5) Eternity in Heaven or Hell. 6) The Coming Judgment.

However, Free Will Baptists have some distinctive doctrines that I think are very important. As we look at these, they will answer the question; Why am I a Free Will Baptist?

Our Doctrine

The Doctrine of Salvation
In order to understand where we are coming from we need to understand what was taking place in this country's beginning. The doctrine of Calvinism was the predominant view of the churches in the early 1700's. This was developed by the great Swiss reformer-John Calvin. The basic beliefs of Calvinism are as follows:

- *Total Depravity*-Man possessed no ability to make a choice about God.
- *Unconditional Election*-Because man had no ability to choose God, before the world was created, God chose those who would be saved and lost.
- *Limited Atonement*-According to Calvin, Christ did not die for the whole world but only for the elect.

- *Irresistible Grace*-If you were one of the chosen, when the call of salvation came, you could not resist the call!
- *Perseverance of the Saints*-Once you were saved you could never lose your salvation which is called "Unconditional Eternal Security."

There are not many five Point Calvinists today but many do hold on to the final point-Unconditional Eternal Security!

I'm glad at this same time there were men like Paul Palmer and Benjamin Randall preaching something else! They did not agree with Calvinism and preached a different doctrine. There were basically two ways that Palmer and Randall disagreed with Calvin.

That all men have a free will to accept or reject the Gospel.

Free Will Baptists have always believed that it was God's intention and desire for all men to be saved. The following scriptures illustrate this.

John 3:16 *For God so loved the world that he gave his only begotten Son that whosoever believeth in him should not perish but have everlasting life.*

Romans 10:13 *For whosoever shall call upon the name of the Lord shall be saved.*

Revelation 22:17 *And the Spirit and the bride say come. And let him that heareth, say come. And let him that is athirst come. And whosoever will, let him come.*

Free Will Baptists have always proclaimed Free Will, Free Grace, and Free Salvation to all who wants it! And they were branded as heretics for preaching this! I am glad they were willing to accept the scorn to preach the truth!

That men in their free will can make shipwreck of their faith.

First of all I would like to say that Christians have much security in Jesus Christ. We are not saying that God is up in heaven just waiting for an opportunity to cut us off when we fail. He is a longsuffering Father who patiently teaches, corrects and disciplines those who are His. We are saying that we cannot willfully walk away from Christ and expect to go to heaven! There are many warnings in the scripture to believers about making shipwreck of our faith.

II Peter 2:20-21 *For if after they have escaped the pollutions of the world through the knowledge of the Lord and Savior Jesus Christ, they are again entangled therein, and overcome, the latter end is worse with them than the beginning. For it had been better for them not have known the way of righteousness, than after they have known it, to turn from the holy commandment delivered unto them.*

Hebrews 3:12 *Take heed, brethren, lest there be in any of you an evil heart of unbelief, in departing from the living God.*

Hebrews 6:4-6 *For it is impossible for those who were once enlightened, and have tasted of the heavenly gift and were made partakers of the Holy Ghost, and have tasted the good word of God and the powers of the world to come, If they shall fall away, to renew them again unto repentance; seeing they crucify to themselves the Son of God afresh, and put him to an open shame.*

Hebrews 10:26-27 *For if we sin willfully after that we have received the knowledge of the truth, there remaineth no more sacrifice for sins.*

Free Will Baptists have always taken the position, that a man does not lose his free will after he is saved and that God will not take anyone to heaven against their own will!

I am a Free Will Baptist because I believe in free will and not predestination or unconditional eternal security.

The Doctrine of Ordinances

An ordinance is a practice of the church that we are "ordained" to perform. We can look at ordinances one of two ways; we can observe them as a *church* ordinance or a *divine* ordinance. What difference does this make? It makes a big difference in the way they are practiced.

There are many churches who practice church ordinances who will not accept the baptism of someone who comes from another Bible believing church. In order to be a member of their church, they must baptize you because it is a church ordinance.

Also, those churches who believe in church ordinances will not serve communion to a believer who is not a member of their church because they believe this is a church ordinance.

Free Will Baptists observe these ordinances as divine ordinances because they did not originate with the church but with Christ Himself.

After all, Jesus gave us direction about baptism in Matthew 28:18b-19 *All power is given unto me in heaven and in earth. Go ye therefore, and teach all nations, baptizing them in the name of the Father, and of the Son, and of the Holy Ghost:* That is why a person who is baptized the way Jesus prescribed is accepted in a FWB Church. We recognized Jesus' authority!

It is the same with communion. Free Will Baptists will welcome to the table any believer in Christ because it was Jesus who instituted the last supper. Luke 22:19 *And he took bread and gave thanks and brake it, and gave it unto them saying; This is my body, which is given for you: this do in remembrance of me.*

There is a third ordinance Free Will Baptists observe--the washing of the saint's feet. Why do we practice feet washing? First of all, the lessons that can be learned by observing this ordinance found in John 13 are enormous.

The first lesson we learn is *Humility*--a greatly needed lesson for today. Just before John 13 we find the disciples in Luke 22 having an argument over who was the greatest. Doesn't this sound just like us? It is ironic that the greatest One among them was the One who girded Himself and performed the humble task none of them wanted to do. What a great lesson for us!

Secondly, we can also learn *Service*. Jesus had sent everyone out of the room except for Himself and the disciples. All the servants who would usually wash their feet were gone. So you had a room full of disciples who had come to *be served* rather than to *serve*. How much does this sound like the modern day church? Many come to church today looking to be served rather than serve. How different it would be if we had a church full of people coming to serve? I believe it would revolutionize our churches if this attitude would prevail!

Lastly, we learn the daily need of *Cleansing*. When Jesus approached Peter to wash his feet, Peter refused. Jesus said that if He didn't wash him, that he had no part with Jesus! Peter relented and asked for Jesus to wash everything. Jesus said that it was not necessary to wash everything, but he did need his feet cleaned. This teaches that when we come to Christ, He cleanses us completely, but we do walk in a dirty world. There are many things in the world that will attach themselves to our feet. It may be a bad attitude, bad habit, a grudge or host of other sins that may seek to cling to us. Feet washing shows me that I must come to Jesus daily to keep my feet clean and not allow these things to soil my relationship with Him.

I will conclude this portion about feet washing by saying: Jesus *did it*, Jesus *commanded* it, the early church *practiced it* and Jesus said we would *be happy if we did it!*

The Doctrine of Baptism

Free Will Baptists believe that baptism is a vital part of the Christian experience. There are three major points about baptism that Free Will Baptists promote.

We practice *Believers Baptism* only. This is why you will see no infants baptized in a FWB Church. We believe that baptism is an outward act that pictures an inward experience. In Acts 8 where Philip preached Jesus to the Ethiopian eunuch, the eunuch asked what was hindering from being baptized. *Philip said If thou believest with all thine heart, thou mayest. And he answered I believe that Jesus is the Son of God.* (Acts 8:37-38) Only when the eunuch professed his faith in Christ would Philip baptize him.

We do not practice *Baptismal Regeneration*. Some teach that you must be baptized in order to be saved. Free Will Baptists never have accepted this, believing that salvation comes *"by grace through faith"* Ephesians 2:8-9.

The thief on the cross in Luke 23 never had the opportunity to be baptized. If Baptismal Regeneration is true, then there are some places on the earth that I could not be saved! I am glad however that there is not a square inch on this earth, where a person who cries out to the Lord cannot be saved!

We will only *baptize by Immersion*. The reason we do this is if you go back to the root words "Baptiso" "Baptizien" they do signify a burial. This is why Biblical baptism is to baptize by immersion.

It is also the only way to show the picture of death and burial in Romans 6. When a person is baptized they are saying that they believe in Christ's death, burial and resurrection. Further, they are saying that they are identifying themselves with His death, burial and resurrection. Immersion is the only mode of baptism that will show this great truth.

The Doctrine of the Baptism of the Holy Spirit
We teach that *Every Christian receives the Holy Spirit at Conversion*. The Holy Spirit comes to live in a believer the moment they receive Christ as Savior.

Look carefully at this verse. I Corinthians 12:13 *For by one spirit are we all baptized into one body, whether we be Jews or Gentiles, whether we be bond or free and have been all made to drink into one spirit.* Notice the word "all" used two times to show that every Christian has been baptized into the body of Christ.

Paul teaches in the book of Romans that you cannot be a Christian without the Spirit. Romans 8:9 *Now if any man have not the Spirit of Christ, he is none of his.*

He further says in the book of Colossians that if you possess Christ, you have the Godhead. (Father, Son, Holy Ghost) Colossians 2:9-10 *For in him dwelleth all the fullness of the Godhead bodily. And ye are complete in him, which is the head of all principality and power.*

It is clear that every believer possesses the Holy Spirit.

We also teach a *Progressive Sanctification* that will be complete when Jesus comes. Sanctification is that process whereby God takes weak, sinful, and mistake prone Christians and makes us like Him. The One who saved us will patiently work with believers. Philippians 1:6 *Being confident of this very thing, that he which hath begun a good work in you will perform it until the day of Jesus Christ.*

When is this process complete? It is found in I John 3:2 *Beloved, now are we the sons of God, and it doth not yet appear what we shall be, but we know that, when he shall appear we shall be like him, for we shall see him as he is.* This is graduation day! On this day temptation will mean nothing. All the failures, problems and trials will be over. We will be like Him!

Doctrine of the Bible

This has always been a vital question and it is most important in the day in which we live. Many churches and denominations are having much controversy over the Bible. I am glad to report that Free Will Baptists are not arguing over the Word of God. We believe:

The Bible is Inspired

We do not look at the Bible as being simply written by men, but we believe that God wrote this book by inspiring men to write it. II Peter 1:21 *For the prophecy came not in old time by the will of man: but holy men of God spake as they were moved by the Holy Ghost.* II Timothy 3:16 *All scripture is given by inspiration of God, and is profitable for doctrine, for reproof, for correction, for instruction in righteousness.*

The Bible is Infallible and Inerrant

We do not teach that the Bible is an error filled book. The best answer I could give to the question, "How do you know the Bible is true?" would be that Jesus said it was! Think of it, when Jesus was on earth the Old Testament was completed. If there were any errors or omissions, He had every opportunity to tell us what they were. Jesus did not do this, rather He said in John 10:35 *The scripture cannot be broken.* He went on to say in Matthew 24:35 *Heaven and earth shall pass away, but my words shall not pass away.* How true this is!

The Bible is our Authority

The authority in a Free Will Baptist Church does not rest in the leaders or hierarchy of the church. It rests firmly on the Word of God! We have all we need for authority in the Word. Our treatise says that the Bible be our "only rule of faith and practice". When men and the Word of God clash in a FWB

Church, we don't get rid of the Word, we get rid of the men! The Bible is the final authority.

The Bible is Complete

We are living in a day where we have a multitude of cults and religious groups telling us that we have missed God's truth and we need their "revelation" to enlighten us. Others are working on their computers looking for some secret Bible code that God has left.

We teach that when you hold the Bible in your hand, you have the completed Word of God. In its pages you will find all you need in how to be saved, to live in this life, to resist temptation and to one day, step on Heaven's shore! When the Lord was directing John to write the book of Revelation, He came to the last chapter and proclaimed a curse for those who would add anything to His Word. In addition, He gives a warning of removing one's name out of the book of life for taking away from His Word Revelation 22:18-19. The Lord has made it clear. The Bible is complete!

With all the religious activity going on, not everyone is valuing doctrinal truth. But I am glad that Free Will Baptists still are! I would rather stand on the truth alone, than to stand on error with the crowd.

Our Government

The local church is the highest authority in our denomination. All ministries are subject to the local churches. No denominational hierarchy has any power over the local congregation. Our churches are self-governing. They hold the deed to their own properties and select their own pastors.

The way I see it, this allows Free Will Baptists the best of both worlds. Our churches have the freedom to minister to their particular area without interference from the denomination, yet at the same time have the vehicle to voluntarily unite with other local bodies to do together what we cannot do alone. (Examples: Missionaries, Bible College, etc.) Not many of our churches would have enough resources to place missionaries on the field, provide a Bible College, or maintain a publishing house, but 2,500 churches can! In our own state, I can see churches like First Austintown, Lancaster, Zanesville, Neville, Hamilton, Ashtabula, and London. These churches were started because the Free Will Baptist churches of the state of Ohio have planted them! It's a wonderful thing to work together for the cause of Christ.

You will see listed below those ministries that Free Will Baptists have united together to support.

National Ministries

Executive Office
National Convention
ONE Magazine
Together Way Giving Program
National Leadership Conference
International Missions
Oversees Missionary Families in Foreign Countries
Home Missions
Oversees Missionary Families in United States, Canada, Mexico, Puerto Rico and Virgin Islands

Welch College
 Trains Ministers, Missionaries, Church Workers, and others who desire a Christian Education
 Retirement Program
 Retirement for Ministers & Full Time Workers
 Randall House Publishing
 Provides Sunday School Literature, Teaching Helps, and Books
 Women National Active For Christ

National Women's Auxiliary to assist our National Ministries and our Churches.

Master's Men

National Men's Auxiliary to assist our National Ministries and our Churches.

Ohio State Ministries

Ohio State Office

State Evangelist, Ambassador Magazine, Ohio Men's Retreat, Together Way Giving Plan, Ohio Bible Institute, Ambassador EBookstore, Pastor to Pastor, Church Assistance Revitalize Your Sunday School Seminar, and Ohio Website, Ohio Email Updates

Ohio State Missions

Supports Mission Work throughout Ohio.

Ohio Youth Conference

Oversees the Youth Ministry of the State

Our Support

How are these ministries funded?
There are two ways to support this ministry.

1. The Co-op Plan. This plan is like tithing to your local church. It is given and distributed as the Ohio State Association has voted on at the State Meeting yearly. When a church gives to the Co-op plan, the offering is divided the following way. 70% of the offering stays in Ohio and are used for our ministries and 30% are sent to Nashville for National ministries. The way the 70% that Ohio ministries will use are divided as follows: 5% goes to the Pastor's Retirement, 47% comes to the State Office for the ministries mentioned above, 15% goes to our State Mission Program, and 3% goes to our State Youth Program.

2. Designated Giving. You also have the option of designating your offering. You can give the percentages that you decided to each individual ministry. You have the option of giving directly to the State Office, Ambassador Magazine, State Missions, State

Youth or any of the National Ministries. All these state and national ministries are worthy of support. Some churches give a combination of Co-op and designated.

As I said earlier, Free Will Baptists have the best of both worlds. We do not have a denomination hierarchy that forces our churches to do what the denomination wants them to. No one comes to our churches and tells us we "have" to give to any ministry. We do however, have the opportunity to voluntarily work with our sister churches "To Do Together What We Cannot Do Alone." I believe that every church should do their part to support Free Will Baptist ministries.

In Conclusion
I hope this has given you a clear answer to the question, "Why I am a Free Will Baptist." Our doctrine, our fellowship and our common purpose hold us to together to be able to accomplish much more than if we could do individually. I am thankful and proud to be called a Free Will Baptist!

www.ingramcontent.com/pod-product-compliance
Lightning Source LLC
Chambersburg PA
CBHW071457040426
42444CB00008B/1383